Prayer Guide For Spiritual Vitality

Nutrients for Spiritual Strength and Growth

MICHAEL A. OLADUNJOYE

Prayer Guide for Spiritual Vitality
Copyright © 2019 by Micheal A. Oladunjoye
All rights reserved.

Requests for information should be addressed to:
micholadunjoye@gmail.com

This book, or parts thereof, may not be reproduced, stored in a retrieval system, or transmitted in any form or by any means, electronic, mechanical, photocopying, recording or otherwise, without the written permission of the publisher.

Scriptures marked KJV are taken from the KING JAMES VERSION (KJV): KING JAMES VERSION, public domain.

Scriptures marked NKJV are taken from the NEW KING JAMES VERSION (NKJV): Scripture taken from the NEW KING JAMES VERSION®. Copyright© 1982 by Thomas Nelson, Inc.
Used by permission. All rights reserved.

Scriptures marked AMP are taken from the AMPLIFIED BIBLE (AMP): Scripture taken from the AMPLIFIED® BIBLE, Copyright © 1954, 1958, 1962, 1964, 1965, 1987 by the Lockman
Foundation Used by Permission

Scriptures marked CEV are taken from the CONTEMPORARY ENGLISH VERSION (CEV):
Scripture taken from the CONTEMPORARY ENGLISH VERSION copyright© 1995 by the American Bible Society. Used by permission.

Scriptures marked NIV are taken from the NEW INTERNATIONAL VERSION (NIV): Scripture taken from THE HOLY BIBLE, NEW INTERNATIONAL VERSION ®. Copyright©
1973, 1978, 1984, 2011 by Biblica, Inc.™. Used by permission of Zondervan

Published By: Achievers World Publishing

ISBN: 978-0-6486778-4-0 (paperback)
ISBN: 978-0-6486778-5-7 (ebook)

Printed in Australia

DEDICATION

To the glory of the Almighty God and the LORD Jesus Christ who called, chose, and gave me the vision. He remains the great motivator for this book.

ACKNOWLEDGMENTS

My reverend worship and special appreciation to the Most High God for sending Jesus Christ at the fullness of time into my life to save my soul, open my eyes, as well as call and choose me for His purpose; to the LORD Jesus Christ, the author of life for giving me the vision and revelation; to the Holy Spirit for the capacity to write and complete this book despite all the compelling factors.

My gratitude also goes to the following people:

My mentor, Dr. D.K. Olukoya, President and Mentor, Goshen Club International for the fire of prayer kindled in me through the Apostolic Fire conferences and the Prayer and Deliverance Bible authored by him.

My wife, Deaconess Victoria Omolola Oladunjoye, my children, Adeyemi and Olawumi Adesanya; Afolabi and Tonbra Oladunjoye; Oluwole and Temidayo Oduneye; Olugbenga and Abisola Eleshinnla; also, to my grandchildren for their encouragement and support in one form or the other and at one time or the other during the process of actualizing this project.

My brothers in Christ, Bayo Adesanya and Pastor Femi Oyewopo for their counsel, inspiration, motivation and especially the efforts to make the project see the light of the day.

My friends, colleagues, children in the Lord, and a host of well-wishers touched by practical ministrations — thank you for the inspiration received through your testimonies and advice to put the knowledge into writing.

It is my sincere hope that, to a large extent, this book fulfils your most valued expectation.

Michael Akin. Oladunjoye

PREFACE

There is no way any book on prayer can claim absolute perfection. The best that can be claimed is that the book is perfect, good, hot, potent or effective but not absolute. I say this because prayer is talking to God about our needs in different ways: praise, worship, thanksgiving, supplication or intercession. It also takes various formats without set rules, patterns or ways of presentation.

When a book on prayer is written to fulfil a purpose and destiny, there is little fear about the format, rule or pattern. The objective is to present the prayers therein as they are revealed. This book, therefore, approaches prayers in line with the pattern in which they were revealed and presented in practical life ministrations.

The cardinal point to emphasize here is that if you intend to pray, try to do it according to the revelation received. When it agrees with the Word of God, leave the answer and supernatural intervention to God Almighty. Also, and most importantly, the person who intends to pray must ensure he or she is in right standing with God. Words of wisdom say, "It is not possible for God to use you as lighthouse anywhere if He cannot use you as candle where you are now."

I hope you will follow the approach taken in this book to achieve the success in your life, which was received and recorded by those who used these prayers in the past.

Anyone who sincerely and faithfully applies these prayers to any need in life can succeed.

Michael Akin. Oladunjoye

Table of Contents

Prayers For Divine Power..................................... 11

Prayer 1: Seek First The Kingdom Of God And
His Righteousness 13

Prayer 2: Connect Me To Your Divine Power
For Extraordinary Exploits.......................................17

Prayer 3: I Shall Rule Over My Enemies 21

Prayer 4: Give Me Oil In My Lamp And Keep
My Light Burning, O Lord.......................................25

Prayer 5: Gird Me With Strength And Make
My Way Perfect, O Lord! 29

Prayers For Divine Protection........................... 33

Prayer 6: Make Me Dwell In Your Secret Place, O Lord 35

Prayer 7: Deliver My Soul From Death, Eyes From
Tears, And Feet From Falling, O Lord!....................39

Prayer 8: Cut Off All The Enemies Of My
Divine Acceleration Unto Greatness, O Lord!..........45

Prayer 9: Burst Through My Enemies Like A Raging
Flood And Sweep Them Away, O Lord! 49

Prayer 10: Be My Strong Habitation, O Lord 53

Prayer 11: Bring Down The Noise Of Strangers
In My Life, O Lord 57

Prayer 12: In Times Like These, Be A Wall Of Fire
Round About Me, O Lord......................................61

Prayer 13: Hide Me In The Shelter Of Your Presence, O Lord! 65

Prayer 14: I Shall Fear No Evil 69

Prayer 15: Be My Sun And Shield, O Lord 73

Prayer 16: Make My Path A Shining Light, O Lord.............. 77

Prayers For Divine Prosperity And Peace 81

Prayer 17: Cast Out All Adversaries From The Great Door You Opened For Me, O Lord!.. 83

Prayer 18: Cancel Every Season Of Lack And Famine In My Life And Family, O Lord!... 87

Prayer 19: Confound My Adversaries With Your Peace And Prosperity In My Life, O Lord!...................................... 91

Prayer 20: Bless And Keep Me, O Lord!............................... 95

Prayer 21: Open Unto Me The Channel Of Your Great Goodness, O Lord 99

Prayer 22: Open Unto Me The Door Of Great Opportunities, O Lord!... 103

Prayer 23: Make Your Face Shine Upon Me, O Lord!........ 107

Prayer 24: Make Me Fruitful In Every Good Work, O Lord! 111

Prayer 25: Compass My Life With Your Season Of Mercy And Favour, O Lord!... 115

Prayer 26: Position Me For Divine Increase, O Lord. 119

Prayer 27: Satisfy Me With Honey Out Of The Rock, O Lord 123

Prayer 28: Make Me Drink Of The River Of Thy Pleasure, O Lord..................127

Prayer 29: Water My Dry Land, O Lord..............131

Prayer 30: Put A New Song Into To Mouth.......135

Prayer 31: Disgrace Every Enemy Of My Divine Comfort, O Lord!................139

Prayer 32: Extend Unto Me Your Peace And Comfort, O Lord!......................143

Destiny Shaping Prayers........................147

Prayer 33: Bring Me Unto My Desired Haven, O Lord......149

Prayer 34: Plant My Feet On Higher Ground, O Lord........153

Prayer 35: Make Me A Good Steward Of Your Manifold Grace, O Lord!......................157

Prayer 36: Make My Life Your Testimony, O Lord............161

Prayer 37: Remember Me, O Lord......................165

Prayer 38: Lift My Head High Above The Reach Of Man, O Lord!................169

Prayer 39: Bring Out The Star In Me And Cause It To Shine Brightly, O Lord!....................173

Prayer 40: Make Me Your Peculiar Treasure, O Lord!........177

Prayer 41: Exalt My Horn With Honour, O Lord! 181

Prayer 42: Lead And Guide Me Unto Greater Heights, O Lord!......................185

Prayer 43: Refine Me As Gold For A Righteous Service To You, O Lord!......................189

Prayer 44: Guide Me With Your Counsel
Continually, O Lord 193

Deliverance And Healing Prayers 197

Prayer 45: Cancel The Plan And Mark Of The Enemy
Over Y My Life, O Lord! 199

Prayer 46: Moving Out The Mountain In My Life
And Casting Same Into The Sea 203

Prayer 47: Rise Up And Scatter Evil Conspiracy
In My Life And Family, O Lord! 207

Prayer 48: Open My Eyes To See Your Great
And Mighty Plan For My Life, O Lord! 211

Prayer 49: Work Your Unforgettable And Marvelous
Work In Me, O Lord 215

Prayer 50: Pull Down Every Satanic Stronghold In
My Life, O Lord! 219

Prayer 51: Utterly Consume All Wicked Pursuers
In My Life With Terrors, O Lord! 223

Prayer 52: Silence The Rage Of The Wicked
In My Life, O Lord! 227

Prayer 53: There Shall Be Showers Of Blessing 231

INTRODUCTION

Then He spoke a parable to them that men always ought to pray and not to lose heart (Luke 18:1, NKJV).

This parable of the LORD Jesus Christ shows the need for all people to persevere in prayer and make it a habit. When Jesus spoke these words, He knew many people in the world had problems: bondage of sin, ignorance, unbelief, demonic and witchcraft powers, vices, poverty, sickness or infirmity, curses, and covenants, to mention a few.

Out of His sincere desire and love to set willing souls free from evil bondage or captivity, Jesus Christ came to the earth, ministered deliverance and healing to people and, indeed, gave His life for the salvation of the entire world. The purpose of salvation is for people to be delivered from the power of darkness and translated into the kingdom of God (Colossians 1:13). From the time of His appearance, Jesus Christ has been searching for people to choose, anoint, and send forth as His instruments to liberate the people from bondage.

Prayer provides the channel for human beings to call upon God for help and access to the divine plan and purpose of God for their provision, prosperity, deliverance, and healing. In other words, prayer is:

i. Simply talking to God anytime and anywhere

ii. Releases the power of God to act

iii. Opens the door for God to work

iv. Helps to draw from the blessings of heaven

v. Provides the way of spiritual vitality

It is written,

> For I know the thought that I think towards you, saith the LORD, thoughts of peace, and not of evil, to give you an expected end. Then shall ye call upon me, and ye shall go and pray unto me, and I will hearken unto you. And ye shall seek me, and find me, when ye shall search for me with all your heart. (Jeremiah 29:11-13, KJV)

God wants to hear our prayers, so He said,

> Ask and it shall be given you: seek and ye shall find; knock and it shall be opened unto you. (Matthew 7:7, KJV)

God is the Creator and source of all things, which flow unto His creatures. God also occupies a unique position and has a distinctive role to play in the affairs of human beings. He possesses the capacity to shape the destiny of human beings for good or otherwise (Daniel 5:21). The concept and importance of prayer, therefore, flow from human beings' need to turn to God for intervention in various aspects of their affairs.

Men have been calling on God from as early as Genesis 4:26; however, the need for and intensity of prayer continue to increase. In response to this need, this prayer manual was written to provide spiritual resources that will bring believers together and usher them into the goodness of the kingdom, as well as connect them through divinely inspired prayers. The kingdom of God and of His Christ is a special place or way of life established by God in which perfect protection, peace, and happiness are enjoyed by those who dwell therein.

The pattern of presentation adopted in this manual is for the prayer topics to be in group form according to the subject matter; this makes it convenient. This grouping includes prayers for power, protection, prosperity, destiny reshaping, restoration, general deliverance, and healing. Specifically,

(a) Prayers for divine power are designed to bring about power, authority, and faith, which are very valuable and greatly required, not only to ensure an effective prayer life but also to sustain believers in Christ in the realm of spiritual and physical victory. The Holy Spirit has been given to impart power. However, He must be allowed to remain in you (the believer), constantly fed and nurtured with the Word of God as you pursue purity and keep Him active by persistent prayers.

(b) Prayers for divine protection are necessary to contain the security challenges and trepidation in the people of the world at the present time. The world is gradually drifting toward global annihilation whereby insecurity reigns supreme. In every nation of the world, conflicts and hostilities have taken over the daily news and reports. Weapons of mass destruction are being developed and tested daily by nations that have acquired such weapons. Satanic wickedness, including terrorism, earthquakes, pestilences, epidemics, and famines in domestic, national, and international spheres have increased. People need to turn to God in prayers for safety and protection.

(c) Prayers for prosperity and peace draw their importance from the tragedy of human life. In the beginning, when God created man (human beings), He said:

Let us make man in our image, after our likeness…And God blessed them, and God said unto them to this end, Be fruitful, and multiply, and replenish the earth, and subdue it: and have dominion over the fish of the sea, and over the fowl of the air, and over every living thing that moveth upon the earth…And God said, Behold, I have given you every herb seed, which is upon the face of all the earth, and every tree, in the which is the fruit of a tree yielding seed, to you it shall be for meat. (Genesis 1:26, 28, 29, KJV)

The above scriptures about creation reveal the mind of God for the prosperity of mankind whom He made. However, due to satanic manipulation and the disobedience of man, sin entered the world; hence, the right to divine prosperity was lost. Even though the LORD Jesus Christ has restored this right to believers in Him, requests for prosperity are directed to God. Through prayers, therefore, all that is needed to make one prosperous can be divinely received when the kingdom of God and its righteousness are made the priority in one's life.

But seek ye first the kingdom of God and his righteousness, and all these things shall be added unto you. (Matthew 6:33)

Ask and it shall be given you; seek, and ye shall find; knock, and it shall be opened unto you. (Matthew 7:7, KJV)

Thus, these prayers will help to draw from the blessings in the heavenly stores for those who ask for them.

(d) Prayers for destiny shaping and restoration draw their importance from the need to wrestle with the wicked people of the world and liberate one's God-ordained destiny from their control. Greatness remains God's plan for every human being.

For thou hast made him a little lower than the angels, and hast crowned him with glory and honour. (Psalm 8:5, KJV)

The psalmist makes it clear that God is the source of all greatness and in creating man He ordained him to be great.

Satanic wickedness operating through demonic and witchcraft powers in the society and families have constituted themselves into ferocious robbers and destroyers of human destinies. Through sin and carelessness, believers in Christ are caught in the web of manipulation by these evil powers. Usually, the aspect of life that attracts their manipulation is human destiny. Those destined for greatness by God live as servants because of such manipulation.

When the God-ordained destiny of anyone is tampered with, such a person cannot accomplish much good in life. Believers in Christ who are caught in these destiny manipulations by the forces of darkness must reach out in prayer for recovery and restoration of their God-given destiny.

(e) Prayers for general deliverance and healing are needed to reverse the pain and punishment of captivity. To be in captivity or bondage is to have your freedom, access, and ability taken away. It is to be restricted against your will. Captivity can be self-induced whereby a person through sin, wrong actions or missteps enters the snare of the fowler or the brutality of the Devil lawfully. In the same way, human beings, through the sin of disobedience or demonic and witchcraft attacks can fall into different kinds of sickness or infirmity. Such sickness or infirmity can be foundational or generational if it has its origin from previous generations. Some covenants and curses that bring serious afflictions to their victims are usually deeply rooted in the family and traceable to past generations.

> Shall the prey be taken from the mighty or the lawful captive delivered? But thus saith the LORD, Even the captives of the mighty shall be taken away and the prey of the terrible shall be delivered; for I will contend with him that contendeth with thee (Isaiah 49:24, 25, KJV)

God's promise here is to deliver His children from every form of captivity. Through the medium of prayers that are strategically directed at the type of captivity, affliction or sickness, God is adequately positioned to deliver completely.

> Then they cry unto the LORD in their trouble, and he saveth them out of their distresses. He sent his word, and healed them, and delivered them from their destructions. (Psalm 107:19,20, KJV)

In each of the subject topics, there is a short introduction to the subject based on the Word of God to ignite the fire of faith and through the assistance of the Holy Spirit, pray the prayers that follow. It will be more rewarding to go through the prayer points several times on several days. When it is accompanied by fasting, the confidence and expectation of God answering those prayers will surely increase.

> And shall not God avenge his own elect, which cry day and night unto him, though he bear long with them? I tell you that he will avenge them speedily (Luke 18:8a, KJV).

The joy of seeing your prayers answered becomes vivid as you grow in faith and trust in the promises of God concerning the subject for which prayers have been made. In the same way, by persistent prayers, we learn to pray effectively.

In any spiritual programme, prayer book or manual, it must be emphasized that no meaningful success can be achieved without the involvement of:

a) The Holy Spirit (Acts 1:8)

b) The Word of God (Hebrews 4.12)

c) The name of Jesus (John 14:14)

d) The blood of Jesus (1 Peter 1:18,19)

e) Faith (Hebrews 11:6)

f) Righteousness (Proverbs 15:29)

g) Patience/ Endurance (Hebrews 6:12)

When these spiritual valuables play active roles in the arsenal of Holy Ghost-inspired and tested prayers, the solution to those multifarious challenges of life and their potency can be confidently guaranteed. As you begin to dig into the gold mine of the Holy Ghost, you shall come out with plenty of gold and you will never be disappointed. In Jesus' mighty name. Amen.

Therefore, this book is presented to wake up and kindle the fire of prayer in you. It will provide the platform for your deliverance and healing for victorious living.

PRAYERS FOR DIVINE POWER

PRAYER 1

SEEK FIRST THE KINGDOM OF GOD AND HIS RIGHTEOUSNESS

BIBLE VERSES: Matthew 6:33; Romans 5:12, 14, 17; John 3:1-8

INTRODUCTION

The kingdom of God is a special place or way of life established by Him in which perfect happiness is found. While Jesus Christ was teaching His disciples about prayer in Luke Chapter 11, He included the need to pray for the coming of the kingdom of God. This teaching has become what we know as the Lord's Prayer. Thus, it is most appropriate because of the importance and benefits of seeking the kingdom of God as a priority at every opportunity we have to pray.

In seeking the kingdom of God through prayer, it is also necessary to know why you are doing it and, indeed, pray to seek and receive the kingdom.

When God created heaven and earth, His plan was to make a kingdom where human beings would have dominion and live happily, perfectly, and eternally. However, human beings lost the kingdom, which had the glory and fellowship with God because of the sin of disobedience initiated by the Devil (Genesis 3; Romans 3:23). Right from the point of separation and throughout the Old Testament times, every attempt of human beings to have their relationship with God restored proved impossible; there was no permanent solution to the problem of sin.

In the fullness of time, God, out of His love for the world, sent His Son Jesus Christ into the world to redeem human beings. By the shedding of His blood and death, Jesus Christ provided the permanent solution for sin and restored the relationship mankind had with God (Galatians 4:4, 5). The restoration was purely by the mercy and grace of God because human beings did not merit it.

The work of grace, redemption, and restoration that came through Jesus Christ had been put in place and the modality for receiving grace was also set out in the Word of God. Anyone who wishes restoration must receive Jesus Christ and believe in His name. Being born again, which is the process of receiving and believing in Jesus Christ, as well as being baptised provides the platform for seeking and entering the kingdom of God.

In praying to seek the kingdom of God and His righteousness, you must: (i) admit you are a sinner in need of a Saviour, (ii) be willing to turn from your sins and ask

God to forgive you, (iii) believe Jesus Christ died for you and rose from the grave, (iv) invite Jesus Christ, through prayer, to come in and be in control of your life, (v) receive Jesus Christ as LORD and Saviour through the Holy Spirit.

As you pray now, expect the touch of the LORD, the kingdom of God, as well as His righteousness and peace to fill your life. In Jesus' mighty name. Amen.

PRAYER POINTS:

1. My LORD and my Redeemer, I bless and honour Your name for Your abundance of mercy and grace.
2. I plead the blood of Jesus Christ for total cleansing and coverage. In the name of Jesus.
3. LORD, forgive me for anything I have done that can lock the door of Your mercy against me and wipe it out of my life by Your blood. In the name of Jesus.
4. Spirits of disobedience and rebellion in my life die by the fire of God. In the name of Jesus.
5. Holy Ghost, tear down every veil of darkness covering my divine vision. In the name of Jesus.
6. Build me up in Your most holy faith, O LORD. In the name of Jesus.
7. Holy Spirit, prepare my heart to receive You and allow You to control my life. In the name of Jesus.

8. Holy Ghost, kindle the fire of my love for God and His Son, Jesus Christ. In the name of Jesus.

9. LORD, I believe Your work on the cross and receive the power to be one of Your children. In Jesus' name.

10. LORD, Jesus Christ, be my Lord and Saviour and take control of my life forever. In the name of Jesus.

11. Open my eyes and ears of understanding to be mindful of Your leading and direction, O LORD. In the name of Jesus.

12. LORD, let Your light of salvation shine into every dark area of my life. In the name of Jesus.

13. Keep me on the path of holiness, righteousness, and peace, O LORD. In the name of Jesus.

14. Let those who seek You and Your kingdom rejoice and be glad in You, O LORD. In the name of Jesus.

15. LORD, I thank You for Your answer to my prayers and the deliverance that is received. In Jesus' name.

PRAYER 2

CONNECT ME TO YOUR DIVINE POWER FOR EXTRAORDINARY EXPLOITS

BIBLE VERSE: Philippians 4:13

INTRODUCTION

Before the electrical wiring of the internal electric network of a building is connected to the external power grid, the entire network is as dead as a doormat. But once the network is connected to the power grid on the external line, the whole building space is charged with power and no part of the network can be toyed with. In the same way, a believer in Christ remains as weak as a weakling until a definite spiritual connection to the divine power of Christ is attained through the Holy Spirit's baptism.

Philippians 4:13, "I can do all things through Christ which strengtheneth me" clearly establishes the foregoing truth. From every account recorded in the Bible on the topic, it demonstrates the futility of every other power anywhere other than that which is derived from Jesus Christ (1 Samuel 28:7, Acts 3:6-9, 2 Peter 1:3-4).

When we recognize the importance of the source to the success of any connection, it informs our focus on praying the following: "I prophesy, therefore, that every source of power other than that of God and Christ shall be frustrated. On the contrary, you shall be connected to all the divine power of Christ and do extraordinary exploits in your spiritual assignment. In Jesus' mighty name. Amen."

PRAYER POINTS

1. Mighty and awesome God, I worship and honour You for Your regular blessings through this programme. May Your most holy name be praised forever. In the name of Jesus.
2. I plead the precious blood of Jesus Christ and soak myself and family in the blood. In the name of Jesus.
3. Powers contending with God's power in my life fall down now and die. In the name of Jesus.
4. LORD, repair every rusty pipe, cable or antenna in my spiritual power connection or replace it. In the name of Jesus.
5. LORD, perfectly and permanently correct any mistakes in my spiritual power connection exposed by my spiritual assignment. In the name of Jesus.

6. LORD, by your fire, chase out any character traits in me that are tampering negatively with the power flow into my spiritual life. In the name of Jesus.

7. Power failure gadgets planted into my power connecting network by remote control power of darkness, be rendered useless. In the name of Jesus.

8. Make me tarry in Your presence for the right spiritual transformation and turn my desire to tarry constantly into power booster in my assignment for You, O LORD.

9. LORD, make it clear to me the battles I do not need to engage in and give me the power to cooperate with Your stand on it. In the name of Jesus.

10. Make me dependable when carrying out your assignments for me. In the name of Jesus.

11. LORD, turn my life around for good and success as you did the lives of Joseph, Mordecai, Daniel, and Paul for good exploits. In the name of Jesus.

12. LORD, bless all those who support me and my family in kind and prayers beyond their wildest imagination. In the name of Jesus.

13. LORD, let Your mighty hand set my own prosperity in motion now as You prospered Abraham, David, and Gaius, our fathers of the faith. In the name of Jesus.

14. Every spirit of counterattack or satanic retaliations over these prayers, be bound and consumed by fire. In the name of Jesus.
15. Lord, I thank You most sincerely for answering these prayers. In the name of Jesus.

PRAYER 3

I SHALL RULE OVER MY ENEMIES

BIBLE VERSES: Judges 11:1 – 11

INTRODUCTION

To rule is to govern, control or direct. Enemies are those who hate, oppose or reject one another. Therefore, to rule over one's enemies is to control, direct or govern those who naturally would not have wanted you to do so (Judges 11:7).

God's purpose for His people is for them to rule the environment (Genesis 1:26) and live in peace (Jeremiah 11:29). However, the impact of the Devil in the world has fatally thwarted this purpose. Enemies are caused by simple disagreements and misconceptions. These enemies can be very vicious or dangerous to the extent of physical elimination. The point of ruling over your enemies is reached when you eventually subdue all those in opposition bringing them under control and in subjection to you.

As believers in Christ, in our spiritual warfare, we have to contend with serious opposition from the kingdom of darkness, that is, the Devil, demons, and his agents. In warfare, you must fight. As you do this through the following prayers using the weapons available and with God and His hosts of heaven on your side, you shall surely win and rule over your enemies. In Jesus' mighty name. Amen.

PRAYER POINTS:

1. My Creator and Redeemer, I worship You for making me fearfully and wonderfully.

2. I plead the blood of Jesus Christ for cleansing and total coverage. In the name of Jesus.

3. Holy Spirit, fill my faith with Your fire. In the name of Jesus.

4. Household witchcraft hands planting seeds of fear and failure into my life, wither and burn to ashes by the fire of God. In the name of Jesus.

5. By Your power, O LORD, take over every aspect of my life not surrendered to you. In the name of Jesus.

6. LORD, open my eyes to see the secret places of the Enemy and to avoid them. In the name of Jesus.

7. Holy Spirit, expose the secret plans of the Enemy and frustrate them. In the name of Jesus.

8. Whatever has been working for the Devil in my family, LORD, expose and destroy it. In the name of Jesus.

9. By Your Spirit, O LORD, lead me into total obedience to Your Word and prosper me in it. In the name of Jesus.

10. Agents of the dark kingdom assigned to torment my peace and good health, be consumed by the fire of God. In the name of Jesus.

11. LORD, be with me and still every storm that may come up on the journey of my life. In the name of Jesus.

12. Release Your divine protection upon me and my family, O LORD. In the name of Jesus.

13. As one of Your children, O LORD, make me dwell in Your secret place. In the name of Jesus.

14. I refuse to abide in the habitation of the wicked but shall abide under the shadow of the Almighty God. In the name of Jesus.

15. LORD, I thank You for Your answer and having You as my secret place and fortress. In the name of Jesus.

PRAYER 4

GIVE ME OIL IN MY LAMP AND KEEP MY LIGHT BURNING, O LORD

BIBLE VERSE: Luke 12:35 (NKJV)

INTRODUCTION

"Get yourself on fire for God and people will watch you burn" (John Wesley) are wisdom words. This is a clear testimony to the fact that believers need the fire of God in their lives for the Christian journey to be worthwhile.

In the Bible verse, our LORD Jesus Christ emphasized the need for His followers to embrace and maintain the tempo, which comes out of the burning light, for their lives to be sustainable until His second coming.

For that matter, as believers and intercessors, we cannot accomplish much for God unless we are red hot for the attack we unleash on the dark kingdom and its hosts. Hence, if we desire to make a success of the great assignment set before us and still be relevant when He comes back, we must heed the instructions of our LORD Jesus Christ: "Let your loins be girded about, and your lights burning." Know also that we cannot expect God to use us as lighthouses somewhere else if He cannot use us as candles right where we are now.

The following prayers will be made to catch afresh or kindle the Holy Ghost fire. While the LORD supplies the oil, the fire will be nourished and sustained to the end. I prophesy, therefore, that every leakage in your spiritual pipe shall be repaired by the LORD and continue to supply the oil to keep your light burning forever. In Jesus' mighty name. Amen.

PRAYER POINTS:

1. My Father and my God, I bless and magnify Your name because You are gracious and ready to perfect all that concerns me.

2. I plead the blood of Jesus Christ for cleansing and total coverage. In the name of Jesus.

3. Holy Ghost, ignite my life and prayers with Your fire. In the name of Jesus.

4. Fire of God, uproot and burn every instrument of household enemies in the foundation of my life. In the name of Jesus.

5. LORD, seal any leakage in my spiritual pipe now. In the name of Jesus.

6. LORD, by your fire, destroy whatever is in my hand that is capable of quenching the light of God in my life. In the name of Jesus.

7. LORD, frustrate every activity of the dark kingdom assigned to put out my light. In the name of Jesus.

8. LORD, touch my spiritual life and repair the damage done to it by familiar spirits. In the name of Jesus.

9. Holy Ghost, blow away any evil wind assigned to put out the fire of the Holy Spirit in my life. In Jesus' name.

10. LORD, tie Your mantle around my waist and cause it to be girded continually. In the name of Jesus.

11. LORD, cause Your oil to flow into my lamp for my light to burn brightly unto the perfect day of Christ. In the name of Jesus.

12. By Your divine presence in my life, my light shall not be put out by sin or Satan. In the name of Jesus.

13. Under the assistance and control of the Holy Spirit, my light shall not only burn brightly but also bring others to Christ. In the name of Jesus.

14. I shall not lose my focus on Christ on the journey of my life. In the name of Jesus.

15. Lord, I thank You for Your prompt answer to these prayers. In the name of Jesus.

PRAYER 5

GIRD ME WITH STRENGTH AND MAKE MY WAY PERFECT, O LORD!

BIBLE VERSE: *Psalm 18:32*

INTRODUCTION

"To gird with strength" simply means "to hold or bind closely together with a belt or powerful object." In other words, it is to supply or make available the capacity to endure and prepare one for action in challenging situations. "To make the way perfect" is "to be wholesome, complete, free from reproach or inadequacies."

The LORD is the only one who gives strength and power to His people (Psalm 68:35) to meet challenges: rough roads to walk in, mountains to climb, and battles to fight without which growth is impossible. The LORD does not leave us alone with our challenges. He stands beside us, teaches, and strengthens us to face them. Also, as our Father in heaven, He is perfect (Matthew 5:48) and able to make His people perfect in Jesus Christ (Colossians 1:28). David, in our Bible verse, testified to this fact. Considering the LORD's truth, there is every reason to agree with him.

Our Christian journey is full of challenging situations even more at this time. It is quite appropriate for us to remind the LORD of His promise to give us strength for the journey and perfect us. I prophesy, therefore, that the LORD shall arise and deal with every weakness and imperfection in our lives, gird us with strength, and make our ways perfect before Him. In Jesus' mighty name. Amen.

PRAYER POINTS:

1. Merciful and everlasting God, I give You honour and praise for what You are set to do in my life. May Your most holy name be praised forever. In the name of Jesus.

2. I plead the blood of Jesus Christ and cover me and all that belongs to me with the blood.

3. Inherited curse of failure in my life, break by the blood of Jesus and die. In the name of Jesus.

4. Blood of Jesus, correct every inherited defect in my spiritual system. In the name of Jesus.

5. Seed of weakness and infirmity in my life, be uprooted by the fire of God. In the name of Jesus.

6. Holy Ghost, dismantle by Your fire the satanic cobweb covering my progress and hindering my perfection. In the name of Jesus.

7. Words or covenant assigned against my prosperity and success, be frustrated. In Jesus' name.

8. Satanic manipulations in my life and destiny, be nullified by the blood of Jesus Christ.

9. Strength of the LORD, my life is before You; possess me forever. In the name of Jesus.

10. Spirit of the Living God, take me unto perfection in Jesus Christ now. In Jesus' name.

11. LORD, continue to be the Captain of Your host in all the battles of my life as You were with our forefather David who never lost a battle. In the name of Jesus.

12. I receive the spirit of power, love, boldness, and a sound mind to succeed in all my endeavours and on this journey. In the name of Jesus.

13. On the journey of life, shame and disgrace shall not be my portion. In the name of Jesus.

14. LORD, frustrate all the activities of the gates of hell to destroy Your church. In the name of Jesus.

15. Gracious LORD, I thank You for Your prompt answer to these prayers. In the name of Jesus.

PRAYERS FOR DIVINE PROTECTION

PRAYER 6

MAKE ME DWELL IN YOUR SECRET PLACE, O LORD

BIBLE VERSES: *Psalm 91:1 – 6*

INTRODUCTION

The secret place of the Most High is the place of God's protection from any form of danger.

Life is unpredictable, that is, anything can happen to anyone at any time or any place. For example, a man called his wife when he was about to leave his office in the evening and asked her to prepare a special meal for him to eat when he got home. On the way home, he gave somebody a lift in his car who turned out to be an armed robber. The robber shot the man and stole the vehicle. The man never got back home or ate the dinner prepared for him. The world is wicked!

As civilization grows, many wicked tendencies also continue to grow. Events such as earthquakes, tremors, tsunamis, famines, accidents of different kinds: vehicle, air, sea, building or fire; robbery, kidnapping, ritual killing, scams, wars, and terrorism to mention but a few are some of the unpredictable things human beings have to contend with at the present time.

The truth is God never promised us a world free from danger (John 16:33). However, He promised to give us His help and protection whenever we face danger (Psalm 23:4). God is a shelter, a refuge when we are afraid. Faith in the almighty God as our protector will make us dwell in His secret place and carry us through all the dangers and fears of life.

To dwell in the secret place of the Most High, you must

(a) Become one of God's children

(b) Obey God and His commandments

(c) Be filled by the Holy Spirit

(d) Have living faith in God

(e) Watch your thoughts, actions, and ways, making them please God

(f) Be holy and righteous

(g) Be prayerful

(h) Trust God to perform what He has promised. God is faithful. He will surely keep His promises and make you dwell in His secret place forever. In Jesus' mighty name. Amen.

PRAYER POINTS:

1. My Creator and Redeemer, I worship You for making me fearfully and wonderfully.
2. I plead the blood of Jesus Christ for cleansing and total coverage, in the name of Jesus.
3. Holy Spirit, fill my faith with Your fire, in the name of Jesus.
4. Household witchcraft hands planting seeds of fear and failure into my life, wither and burn to ashes by the fire of God, in the name of Jesus.
5. By Your power, O LORD, take over every aspect of my life not surrendered to you, in the name of Jesus.
6. LORD, open my eyes to see the secret places of the enemy and to avoid them, in the name of Jesus.
7. Holy Spirit, expose the secret plans of the enemy and frustrate them, in the name of Jesus.
8. Whatever has been working for the devil in my family, LORD, expose and destroy it, in the name of Jesus.
9. By Your Spirit, O LORD, lead me in total obedience to Your Word and prosper me in it, in the name of Jesus.

10. Agents of dark kingdom assigned to torment my peace and good health, be consumed by the fire of God, in the name of Jesus.

11. Whatever storm that may come up on the journey of my life, LORD, be with me and still every storm, in the name of Jesus.

12. Release Your divine protection upon me and my family, O LORD, in the name of Jesus.

13. As one of Your children, O LORD, make me dwell in Your secret place, in the name of Jesus.

14. I refuse to abide in the habitation of the wicked but shall abide under the shadow of the Almighty God, in the name of Jesus.

15. LORD, I thank You for Your answer and having You as my secret place and fortress, in the name of Jesus.

PRAYER 7

DELIVER MY SOUL FROM DEATH, EYES FROM TEARS, AND FEET FROM FALLING, O LORD!

BIBLE VERSES: Psalm 116:8, 9 (NKJV)

INTRODUCTION

Psalm 116 is the psalmist's prayer of praise for deliverance by the LORD. Before the facts contained in the prayer became that of praise, it must have been a prayer of supplication. Therefore, making part of the prayer our focus cannot be a cheap thing at all. In Psalm 56:13, the psalmist used the same words, while Elihu, one of the friends of Job, emphasized the point in his words to Job (Job 33:30).

When we consider the situation in our societies, communities, cities and, indeed, nations of the world at the present time, we notice that the life expectancy has gone down to a very serious level. Several recently discovered diseases and epidemics unknown to the society have surfaced; security challenges are everywhere; disasters of ravaging fire and floodwaters occur In many parts of the earth. These and many other elements have taken a serious toll on the life expectancy of human beings. Hence, we can sum it all up in the statement: "Life is cheap."

The Devil, his demons (fallen angels), and human agents are the enemies of God's children. They carry out their work as revealed by Jesus Christ in John 10:10a – to steal believers' blessings; kill them prematurely and destroy their benefits on the earth, as well as rewards in heaven. These evil works are carried out through organized battles or attacks against believers either in the physical or spiritual.

Truly, as God's children, believers must not fear any evil (Psalm 23:4) or the Devil and his agents. However, God's children must live and abide by the rules and instructions under which God's family operates – to be obedient, holy, righteous, have faith, and trust God. God, the head, will keep His part of the relationship (Psalm 81:10-14; Isaiah 25:8; 1 Samuel 2:9).

In recognition of the power of the LORD to deliver and sustain His own in good living and long life, which the psalmist experienced, we will use part of his prayer of praise in the following prayers. I prophesy, therefore, that the LORD shall arise and use everything that makes Him God to deliver your soul from death, eyes from tears and feet from falling. In the mighty name of Jesus. Amen.

PRAYER POINTS:

1. LORD, God Almighty, I magnify Your most holy name and greatness. Receive all praise and adoration forever. In the name of Jesus.

2. I plead the blood of Jesus for total cleansing and coverage. In the name of Jesus.

3. Holy Ghost fire and power come upon me afresh. In the name of Jesus.

4. Powers of my father's house assigned to block the channel of God's goodness in my life, die by fire! In the name of Jesus.

5. Foundational curse of failure and shame in my life, break and be nullified by the blood of Jesus. In Jesus' name.

6. Every conspiracy of the dark kingdom together with physical enemies to terminate my life prematurely, Holy Ghost thunder, scatter and destroy them. In the name of Jesus.

7. Seeds of terminal sickness planted in my life in the dream, Holy Ghost fire uproot and burn them to ashes. In the name of Jesus.

8. Covenant of untimely death entered by anyone for my life, blood of Jesus, break and cancel it. In the name of Jesus.

9. Whatever the Enemy has programmed into my life and family to cause tears, LORD, wipe it out by Your blood. In the name of Jesus.

10. Every snare of the fowler prepared for my life – fire of God consume it and its owner to ashes. In the name of Jesus.

11. Any power or anyone who is not comfortable with my progress spiritually or physically, you are a liar. Be disgraced out of my life and perish in your evil plan. In the name of Jesus.

12. Spiritual and physical robbers in my life and family, be exposed and die. In the name of Jesus.

13. LORD, wipe out the battles from the dark kingdom against my peace and progress by Your ambush. In the name of Jesus.

14. Any bondage or captivity prepared for my life, catch your owner and perish there. In the name of Jesus.

15. Wonderful LORD, use all that makes You God to deliver my soul from death, my eyes from tears and my feet from falling. In the name of Jesus. (Repeat this point 3 times).

16. Power to always attract divine goodness, benefits, and rewards, fill my life now. In Jesus' name.

17. LORD, renew Your covenant of good health and long life for me and every member of my family. In the name of Jesus

18. Gracious and omnipotent God, I thank You for answering these prayers. In the name of Jesus.

PRAYER 8

CUT OFF ALL THE ENEMIES OF MY DIVINE ACCELERATION UNTO GREATNESS, O LORD!

BIBLE VERSE: 2 Samuel 7: 9 (NKJV).

INTRODUCTION

"Divine acceleration" and "greatness" mean "heavenly speed" and "fame," while "enemies" are "those who oppose or carry out all kinds of evil against another." Therefore, when we ask the LORD to cut off all enemies of divine acceleration unto greatness, we are asking Him for the total elimination of all those who work against God-given progress and fame in our lives.

David, in our Bible verse for today, had the privilege of receiving prompt answers to his requests to be of service to God, that is, to build a house for God. God's answer contained wonderful revelations of victory over all enemies and a covenant of an eternal dynasty for David (2 Samuel 7:16).

The story of David is one that testifies of the plan and purpose of God for human beings. Early in life, David displayed strong love for God (singer), boldness (killed a lion, bear, and even Goliath), and painstaking courage (endured hardness and struggled against Saul, 1 Samuel 16:18; 2 Samuel 17:34-37; 26:6-12). Such qualities, as well as Christ-likeness and the fruit of the Spirit in us, will no doubt endear us to God in this end time when He is looking for such people to depend upon (Ezekiel 22:30).

Realizing this end-time need for God informs the importance of tarrying before God in this month's programme to receive the same grace and favour necessary to meet God's expectations and promotions. I prophesy that the LORD shall renew your love for Him, embolden you, and grant you the capacity to be used by Him, while all the enemies of your divine speed and fame are cut off. In Jesus' mighty name. Amen.

PRAYER POINTS:

1. LORD God Almighty, I worship You and bless Your most holy name for the grace, power, and providence in my life and family. Receive all praise and adoration. In the name of Jesus.

2. I plead the blood of Jesus Christ for total cleansing and coverage for my family and me. In the name of Jesus.

3. LORD, clothe me and my family with unshakable faith and fire. In the name of Jesus.

4. Holy Ghost, with Your fire, dry up every evil flow of idolatry, impurity, and wickedness in my foundation. In the name of Jesus.

5. LORD, frustrate and destroy every plan and design of domestic witchcraft to confuse, delay, and destabilize my divine acceleration unto greatness.

6. Holy Ghost, with Your fire, dismantle every generational barrier or object of distraction on my Christian journey. In the name of Jesus.

7. Holy Ghost, with Your thunder, break to pieces all devices or instruments the enemies are using to monitor my life and destiny. In the name of Jesus.

8. Blood of Jesus, wipe out every evil mark placed upon me in the dream by the Enemy to facilitate his operation in my life.

9. According to Your words, O LORD, lift up my hands upon my adversaries and cut off all the enemies of my divine acceleration unto greatness. In the name of Jesus.

10. My life, receive power and authority for divine acceleration unto God-ordained greatness. In the name of Jesus.

11. LORD, make me untouchable and unstoppable on my journey to Your greatness. In the name of Jesus.

12. O LORD, make us blessings to our generation in the position of greatness prepared for us. In the name of Jesus.

13. By Your divine power, O LORD, change the story of my life into the glory of Your kingdom. In the name of Jesus.

14. Build Your wall of fire around me, O LORD, and keep me as the apple of Your eye. In the name of Jesus.

15. Wonderful LORD, I thank You for answering my prayers by fire. In the name of Jesus.

PRAYER 9

BURST THROUGH MY ENEMIES LIKE A RAGING FLOOD AND SWEEP THEM AWAY, O LORD!

BIBLE VERSE: *2 Samuel 5:20 (NLT)*

INTRODUCTION

To burst through is to appear or come suddenly and forcefully. A raging flood is one that comes violently or forcefully. A violent, raging flood will, as a matter of natural impact, move everything along its path. Therefore, for the LORD to burst through your enemies like a raging flood and sweep them away means there is an extraordinary appearance of heavenly hosts to attack and clear out every adversary standing up to contend with the children of God.

At various times, God's Word describes God as awesome (Deuteronomy 7:21, NKJV), a whirlwind (Nahum 1:3), a raging flood (2 Samuel 5:20), and a consuming fire (Hebrews 12:29) to mention a few. In line with His character, at various times in His Word, God promised to fight battles on behalf of His children in return for their obedience to Him. True to His nature, every promise made in the Bible was performed (Exodus 14:12; 23:22; 2 Chronicles 20:15).

As believers in Christ, it is appropriate for us to request in prayer that the LORD acts in His character, nature, and power to root out our enemies before us. Therefore, as you pray, I prophesy that the LORD shall burst through your enemies like a raging flood and sweep them away. In Jesus' mighty name. Amen.

PRAYER POINTS:

1. Everlasting and awesome God, I bless and honour You for the demonstration of Your mighty power in my life. May Your most holy name be praised forever. In the name of Jesus.

2. I plead the blood of Jesus Christ, as well as soak and cover myself with His blood. In the name of Jesus.

3. Release Your fire and scatter every conspiracy of the dark kingdom over my life. In the name of Jesus.

4. Ancestral powers of my father's house supervising affliction in my life, die by the fire of God. In the name of Jesus.

5. Whatever weapons my enemies are relying on to attack me, LORD, render them impotent. In the name of Jesus.

6. By the authority in the name of Jesus, I paralyze every evil strongman in my life and render their words ineffective. In the name of Jesus.

7. Holy Ghost, answer by your thunder and fire the demonic power of initiation calling my spirit into satanic meetings. In the name of Jesus.

8. LORD, burst through my enemies like a raging flood and sweep them away. In the name of Jesus.

9. By Your divine plan, O LORD, frustrate the plans and agenda of the enemies over my life. In the name of Jesus.

10. With an overrunning flood, O LORD, make an utter end of the dwelling place of my enemies. In the name of Jesus.

11. Set Your angels of torment and destruction against all the stubborn pursuers of my life. In the name of Jesus.

12. Lay Your hands of protection and preservation upon me and every member of my family. In the name of Jesus.

13. Build Your wall of fire around me and everything that belongs to me. In the name of Jesus.

14. Renew Your everlasting covenant of mercy and favour with me. In the name of Jesus.

15. LORD, I thank You for answering these prayers by fire. In the name of Jesus.

PRAYER 10

BE MY STRONG HABITATION, O LORD

BIBLE VERSE: Psalm 71:3

INTRODUCTION

Habitation is any structure designed as a place of dwelling, rest, and a shield from the sun, storm or rain. Most importantly, it is a place of security and peace. Therefore, for the LORD to be one's strong habitation means the LORD is a shield, refuge or fortress (all forms of protection).

The psalmist in our Bible verse is aware of the LORD's perfect protection, hence, his cry unto Him to do what He alone can do. This fact is also confirmed in the book of Proverbs, "The name of the LORD is a strong tower; the righteous run to it, and are safe" (Proverbs 18:10, NKJV). Are you righteous? In other words, are you in right standing with the LORD? Know this fully well that only those in right standing with God can be bold enough to ask the LORD to be their strong habitation.

Every believer in Christ must be persuaded by the evidence in God's Word of the omnipotence of the LORD. They should take advantage of this to maximize the kingdom benefits knowing fully that "Whatever you ask the Father in My name He will give you" (John 16:23, NKJV). These prayers will provide the opportunity to ask the LORD (or renew the request) for protection, which is essential at this time because "The days are evil" (Ephesians 5:16). Therefore, I prophesy that the LORD GOD Almighty shall hear your prayers, dismantle every embargo of darkness built against you, consume with His fire the spirit of fear assigned to torment you, and henceforth be your strong habitation. In Jesus' mighty name. Amen.

PRAYER POINTS:

1. Most righteous Father, I worship You for the assurance of victory in my prayers.
2. I confess every shortcoming in my life and plead the blood of Jesus Christ to nullify it. In Jesus' name.
3. LORD, frustrate every satanic agitation over Your grace upon my life. In the name of Jesus.
4. LORD, dismantle every other habitation set up by the kingdom of darkness to confuse God's plan and protection for me. In the name of Jesus.
5. O LORD, be my refuge and strength. In the name of Jesus.

6. LORD, increase my faith and confidence in Your everpresent help in trouble. In the name of Jesus.

7. Be my rock and fortress, O LORD. In the name of Jesus.

8. LORD, bring my love for You into perfection and cast every fear out of my life. In Jesus' name.

9. LORD, make my home the palace of Your peace and glory. In the name of Jesus.

10. Keep me as the apple of Your eye, O LORD. In the name of Jesus.

11. O LORD, build Your wall of fire around me and all that belongs to me. In the name of Jesus.

12. LORD, preserve my outgoings and incomings now and forever. In the name of Jesus.

13. LORD, fill me with more knowledge of Your care over me so I will not cease to praise You. In the name of Jesus.

14. Be my strong habitation, O LORD, and hasten Your promise of protection to perform it. In the name of Jesus.

15. LORD, I thank You for Your prompt answer to my prayers. In the name of Jesus.

PRAYER 11

BRING DOWN THE NOISE OF STRANGERS IN MY LIFE, O LORD

BIBLE VERSES: *Isaiah 25:5; Psalm 31:18*

INTRODUCTION

"Noise" is a sound, especially a loud one. It may be of fireworks. It may also mean to spread rumours or information around e.g. gossip, blackmail, etc.

Noise can be positive (good) or negative (bad) depending on the motive of the maker and the purpose of the noise. For the purpose of this prayer topic, we are concerned with the negative (bad) aspect of noise, which, more often than not, the enemies will use to destroy their victims. Employing noise in a negative way includes criticism, backbiting, railing, character assassination or verbal wars, among others, which are aimed at inflicting severe injuries on victims of such noises.

The Bible verses, which are part of the prophet Isaiah's prayer-song, clearly demonstrate the ability of God to fight for His own when they do not have the opportunity to be present at the scene of the enemies' noise to plead or fight. Hence, these prayers will create the platform to reach out to the Most High. God's desire for us all is to "Lead a quiet and peaceable life in all goodness and reverence" (1 Timothy 2:2, NKJV). Our God is good, all the time. I prophesy, therefore, that every noise of strangers in your life shall be silenced. In Jesus' mighty name. Amen.

PRAYER POINTS:

1. Heavenly Father, I bless Your most holy name for the victory You will give me today.

2. I plead the blood of Jesus Christ for total cleansing and coverage. In the name of Jesus.

3. Arise, O God and scatter every conspiracy and evil gathering against my life. In the name of Jesus.

4. Every instrument of disreputation and death designed for my life, be wasted by the fire of God. In the name of Jesus.

5. LORD, deliver me from the noise of strangers and from those who persecute me. In the name of Jesus.

6. Put to silence every lying lip, which speaks grievous things proudly and contemptuously against me. In the name of Jesus.

7. Let them be turned back and brought to confusion that devise my hurt by their evil noises. In the name of Jesus.

8. I nullify by the blood of Jesus Christ every contrary noise made against my life. In the name of Jesus.

9. I prophesy that the counsel of the Enemy over my life shall not stand or come to pass. In the name of Jesus.

10. My voice shall prevail over the noise of my enemies. In the name of Jesus.

11. By Your unfailing mercies, O LORD, deliver me from every difficult situation or circumstance programmed into my life. In the name of Jesus.

12. LORD, lay Your mighty hands on me and wipe out every sickness or infirmity. Heal me now. In the name of Jesus.

13. O LORD, bring down the noise of strangers and mockers in my life. Silence them! In the name of Jesus.

14. In Your usual nature, O LORD, remember me in Your plan to prosper me. In the name of Jesus.

15. LORD, I thank You for answers to these prayers and victory received. In the name of Jesus.

PRAYER 12

IN TIMES LIKE THESE, BE A WALL OF FIRE ROUND ABOUT ME, O LORD

BIBLE VERSE: Zechariah 2:5

INTRODUCTION

A wall is a structure put in place for protection from external attacks on those within the coverage of the wall. A wall of fire, therefore, is the structure or wall itself being represented by the burning fire. The burning fire as a wall, not only serves the purpose of protection very well, but it also has the capacity to leave an intruder seriously devastated or consumed, that is, wiped out completely.

In times like these, the security of lives and properties has become an illusion (no longer there). Vices such as international and local terrorism, hired, sectarian, ritual, and extra-judicial killings, robberies, rapes, and kidnappings, to mention just a few, have overtaken the world in unprecedented dimensions. These brutal crimes have brought precious lives and valuable edifices to sudden and untimely destruction.

In the Bible verse, God's promise of protection for Jerusalem and those residing within her is also available to every believer (a child of God) who will call upon the LORD. Hence, the following prayers are designed to provide the platform to call upon God, a consuming fire (Hebrews 12:29), to be the wall of fire (protection) around us from now and unto the end. I prophesy, therefore, that the almighty God shall be a wall of fire round about you and consume all your adversaries by His fire. In Jesus' mighty name. Amen.

PRAYER POINTS:

1. LORD, God Almighty, I honour and worship You for all You are set to do in my life.

2. I plead the blood of Jesus Christ for cleansing and total coverage. In the name of Jesus.

3. Holy Ghost fire, incubate me for the spiritual warfare now. In the name of Jesus.

4. Blood of Jesus, break the hold of any generational curse or powers over my life. In the name of Jesus.

5. LORD, increase the intensity of Your fire operating in and around my life. In the name of Jesus.

6. LORD, burn every satanic stronghold in my life with Your fire. In the name of Jesus.

7. Every conspiracy of the Enemy designed to quench the fire of God in and around me, Holy Ghost thunder scatter them. In the name of Jesus.

8. Every life, property or prosperity destroyer in my life be destroyed by the fire of God. In Jesus' name.

9. LORD, as a consuming fire, clean up every evil deposit in and around my dwelling place. In Jesus' name.

10. Agents of oppression and discomfort in my life, be disgraced. In the name of Jesus.

11. With all that makes You God break the power of destiny diverters in my life. In the name of Jesus.

12. Do the uncommon miracle that will advertise Your name in my life to silence my enemies now. In the name of Jesus.

13. According to Your Word, O LORD, be a wall of fire round about me. In the name of Jesus.

14. I prophesy the LORD shall establish me and my home in all righteousness. I shall be far from oppression; nothing shall make me afraid. Terror shall not come near my home. In the name of Jesus.

15. Wonderful Father, I thank You for answering these prayers by fire. In the name of Jesus.

PRAYER 13

HIDE ME IN THE SHELTER OF YOUR PRESENCE, O LORD!

BIBLE VERSE: Psalm 31:20

INTRODUCTION

The shelter of God's presence is the safe and comfort realm of the Almighty God. To pray that the LORD hides you in the shelter of His presence, therefore, is to ask that you are kept under the watchful eyes of God and enjoy the ultimate divine protection and care.

The psalmist says, "God is our refuge and strength, a very present help in trouble" (Psalm 46:1). This is a clear testimony of the safety, comfort, and care, which the presence of God provides. Currently, the world is characterized by natural disasters, calamities, terrorism, ritual killings, kidnappings, and hostage-taking, robberies, and other social vices. The overall effect is the creation of a serious state of insecurity in people's lives and properties. Matthew 24:6-7 warns of the end time signs and syndrome.

Believers in Christ are expected to discern the times to understand the present trends in global conflicts and be able to stand up in prayer committing their safety into the hands of the unfailing presence of God Almighty. In essence, this is the objective of these prayers. Therefore, I prophesy that the LORD shall stand up, contend with all evil conspirators in your life and keep you safe in the shelter of His presence. In Jesus' mighty name. Amen.

PRAYER POINTS:

1. Mighty and powerful God, I give you praise and worship for Your unfailing love in my life over the years. Receive all adoration and thanksgiving. In the name of Jesus.

2. I plead the blood of Jesus Christ and soak myself in the blood. In the name of Jesus.

3. Holy Ghost, with Your fire, chase out anything in me that offends You. In the name of Jesus.

4. Holy Ghost, rekindle my life and prayers with Your fire. In the name of Jesus.

5. Power from my foundation that seeks to kill the champion spirit in me, die by the fire of God. In the name of Jesus.

6. LORD, command the evil hunters of my life to fall into the snare, which they have set for me. In the name of Jesus.

7. LORD, expose and frustrate every plan and agenda of evil conspirators in my life. In the name of Jesus.

8. LORD, shield me from the wicked ones who are violently opposed to me. In the name of Jesus.

9. LORD, silence the evil tongues of those who strive with me. In the name of Jesus.

10. LORD, hide me in the shelter of Your presence and nourish me there. In the name of Jesus.

11. LORD, as You keep me secure in the shelter of Your presence, fill me with the fullness of Your joy and pleasures also. In the name of Jesus.

12. By faith, I run into the strong tower of the name of the LORD and remain safe. In the name of Jesus.

13. LORD, compass me roundabout with songs of deliverance. In the name of Jesus.

14. By Your mighty power, LORD, intervene in the lives and situations of Your children who are looking up to You. In the name of Jesus.

15. LORD, I thank You for answering these prayers by fire. In the name of Jesus.

PRAYER 14

I SHALL FEAR NO EVIL

BIBLE VERSES: Psalm 91:1 – 16

INTRODUCTION

In our world, evil is everywhere. The word "evil" means anything that is bad, sinful, morally reprehensible, which brings sorrow, distress, and misfortune. Recent happenings around us and to a very large extent in the entire world, attest to the ugly trend of evil. No doubt, the world is full of evil and moving fast towards the consummation of things (Matthew 24:6-8).

As God's children, we need not fear any evil. However, we must maintain a close connection with God and dwell in His secret place (Psalm 91:1). This can be accomplished by studying and meditating on God's Word (the Bible), trusting God and His promises (Isaiah 43:1-5), living righteously (do what is right always), and back everything up with serious prayers (Luke 18:1). Ephesians 6:10-14 enjoins us not to be silent against evil and its source – the Devil. Without God, no one is capable of avoiding evil. As God's children, we are not alone in our battle against evil.

When the things discussed above are in place, you can boldly affirm, "I will fear no evil" (Psalm 23:4). Hence, the following prayers will keep us standing on the solid ground of God and His protection at all times. I prophesy that the LORD shall build His wall of fire around you, and you shall not fear any evil. In the mighty name of Jesus.

PRAYER POINTS:

1. Most High God, I worship and adore You for Your awesome power to protect from evil.

2. I plead the blood of Jesus Christ for cleansing and coverage. In the name of Jesus.

3. Blood of Jesus, flush out and destroy any problem transferred into my life from the womb. In the name of Jesus.

4. I break and loose myself from every inherited curse of evil. In the name of Jesus.

5. O LORD, send Your axe of fire into the foundation of my life and destroy every evil seed of fear planted there. In the name of Jesus.

6. Blood of Jesus, nullify every covenant of evil made on my behalf or by me unconsciously. In Jesus' name.

7. I render every instrument of fear and torment fashioned by the Enemy against me impotent in their hands. In the name of Jesus.

8. Every projection of evil into my life and destiny by wicked powers be frustrated and destroyed. In the name of Jesus.

9. All those planning evil and wickedness against me, I command their evil and wickedness to fall on their heads. In the name of Jesus.

10. I command confusion upon all warfare prepared against my peace. In the name of Jesus.

11. Every power preventing the perfect will of God from being done in my life, receive the judgment of defeat. In the name of Jesus.

12. I command every spirit of death and hell to loose your hold upon my life. In the name of Jesus.

13. O LORD, frustrate and cancel whatever is not Your plan and agenda presently operating in my life. In the name of Jesus.

14. Plant Your seeds of holiness, righteousness, and peace in my heart. In the name of Jesus.

15. LORD, I thank You for prompt answers to my prayers. In the name of Jesus.

PRAYER 15

BE MY SUN AND SHIELD, O LORD

BIBLE VERSE: Psalm 84:11

INTRODUCTION

The "sun" is one of the creations of God, ordained in the beginning to provide greater light to the earth. Also, the "shield" is a broad piece of metal object carried for protection. For the LORD God to be your sun and shield is to have the LORD God as the source of illumination and the object of protection.

The LORD God is "all-powerful" (almighty). The psalmist said of Him, "He is my refuge and fortress...his truth shall be my shied and buckler" (Psalm 91:2, 4). Like the psalmist, it is necessary for us (believers) to fully appreciate God's stand in our lives. God does not promise a world free from danger, but He promises His help whenever we face danger in this most unsecure world .

It must be pointed out, however, that the only reason the LORD God will abandon His assignment and remove His presence is when the believer rejects God and delves into the sin of idolatry. Such a one needs to repent, forsake the sinful ways, and return to the LORD God for the relationship to continue.

In the Bible verse, the psalmist's affirmation of what the LORD God is capable of and is willing to do is a source of inspiration for us to reach out to the LORD God in these prayers and ask Him to do what He only can do – deliver to the uttermost. I prophesy, therefore, that the LORD God shall be your sun and shield. No evil shall befall you. You shall be far from oppression. You shall not fear any evil, and terror shall not come near you. In the mighty name of Jesus Christ. Amen.

PRAYER POINTS:

1. Heavenly Father, I worship You and exalt Your most holy name above the heavens.

2. I plead the blood of Jesus Christ for cleansing and coverage. In the name of Jesus.

3. I stand against any power planning to resist my prayers today and release the consuming fire of God upon it. In the name of Jesus.

4. Every embargo of darkness placed upon my life and destiny, be dismantled by the fire of God. In the name of Jesus.

5. Every satanic veil of darkness covering my dreams and visions, be turned off and be burnt by fire. In the name of Jesus.

6. Demonic cloud covering the sunlight of my glory, I command you to clear out now. In the name of Jesus.

7. LORD, by Your fire, consume all witchcraft power blocking the glory of God in my life. In the name of Jesus.

8. Confound the Enemy of my progress with the grace of Your presence in my life. In the name of Jesus.

9. Let the sun of peace and gladness shine upon my life, O LORD. In the name of Jesus.

10. Silence every evil storm raging in my life and cause it to cease forever. In the name of Jesus.

11. O God, be God in my life and swallow up all my predicaments and fears. In the name of Jesus.

12. With all that makes You God, be my sun and shield, O LORD. In the name of Jesus.

13. LORD, strengthen Your covenant of protection over me. In the name of Jesus.

14. Since no one can delay or stop the sun, the moon and the stars from functioning, I command every

form of delay to my prosperity to vanish. In the name of Jesus.

15. Wonderful LORD, I thank You for answers to my prayers. In the name of Jesus.

PRAYER 16

MAKE MY PATH A SHINING LIGHT, O LORD

BIBLE VERSE: Proverbs 4:18

INTRODUCTION

Light is anything that illuminates, manifests, and reveals. A shining light is the perfect state of light.

God is light (1 John 1:5). His children are expected to be the children of light (Ephesians 5:8a). To pray or ask the LORD to make your path a shining light, therefore, is for you to have the presence of God continually providing perfect illuminations on your way.

The Bible is clear about the fact that the entire world lies in wickedness (1 John 5:19b). It gropes (wanders) in the noonday as in the night (Job 5:14), and darkness covers the earth (Isaiah 60:2a). Hence, those who walk therein have the tendency to drift in confusion, problems, and disasters. As children of God (believers in Christ), we are expected to walk in the light and as the children of light (Ephesians 5:8b). However, due to diverse manipulations of the dark kingdom and its demons, it becomes difficult to attain the expectation and where it is possible it cannot be sustained for a long time.

The objective here is to provide the platform to deal with those things that war against the righteousness of God in us. Moreover, it is for us to seek divine means by which our Christian journey cannot only be free from darkness but also be perfected in light. Therefore, I prophesy that every plan or design of the dark kingdom on your life and journey shall be destroyed, and the LORD God Almighty shall continue to make your path a shining light. In Jesus' mighty name. Amen.

PRAYER POINTS:

1. Everlasting Father, King of Glory, I give You praise, glory, honour, and thanksgiving for Your grace upon my life.

2. By Your unfailing mercies, overlook all my shortcomings, O LORD, and create in me a perfect heart. In the name of Jesus.

3. I plead the blood of Jesus Christ for cleansing and total coverage. In the name of Jesus.

4. O God, descend in Your power upon me mightily now, to contend with every move of the dark kingdom to truncate my journey in life. In the name of Jesus.

5. Ancestral or generational curse that is keeping me wandering and confused in my dream, be broken and cancelled by the blood of Jesus Christ. In the name of Jesus.

6. Holy Ghost, destabilize the powers of the dark kingdom assigned to manipulate my life's journey. In the name of Jesus.

7. Spirit and power of confusion assigned against my life and destiny, receive double destruction of fire. In the name of Jesus.

8. Holy Ghost fire, burn to ashes any property of the dark kingdom in my hand. In the name of Jesus.

9. Send out Your light, O LORD, and let it lead me in the journey of life. In the name of Jesus.

10. As I obey Your Word, O LORD, let it be unto me as the light that is shining in a dark place and as the daystar arising in my heart. In the name of Jesus.

11. O LORD, arise now, subdue every impediment and make my path a shining light. In the name of Jesus.

12. Righteous Father, let Your mighty light swallow up every dark spot in my journey of life. In Jesus' name.

13. Make thy face to shine upon me and cause me to dwell in Your light continually. In the name of Jesus.

14. I prophesy that on my journey in life, I will refuse the inheritance of the wicked. In the name of Jesus.

15. LORD, I thank You for answering these prayers by Your fire. In the name of Jesus.

PRAYERS FOR DIVINE PROSPERITY AND PEACE

PRAYER 17

CAST OUT ALL ADVERSARIES FROM THE GREAT DOOR YOU OPENED FOR ME, O LORD!

BIBLE VERSE: *1 Corinthians 16:9*

INTRODUCTION

An open door spiritually signifies the beginning of new opportunities or the starting point of new efforts that present progress and potential success. To have a great and effectual door opened for you by the LORD means the beginning of good things that lead to success or breakthroughs in your life. It must be emphasized here that the great door opened to us by the authority of the LORD (Revelation 3:7) is salvation, which leads us into His kingdom. From there, other doors of opportunities begin to open.

Faith in the Word of God and prayers are the key channels for getting great and effectual doors (sure opportunities) to open. When a door of new opportunities is opened and you enter, it signifies the beginning of a new experience, which is more often than not a very good and profitable one.

Satan is real. He is called "the god of this world" (2 Corinthians 4:4) and "the prince of the power of the air" (Ephesians 2:2). Satan, his demons (fallen angels), and human agents are the adversaries of man. In some ways, they work principally by deceit and attack to draw people away from God's blessings. Satan is never going to let people get any breakthrough willingly. It is not his nature to just allow a person to freely receive any good opportunities or success. Many of the difficulties that prevent people from accomplishing God's work can be attributed to satanic works (Isaiah 14:17).

Many times, something has to be broken in the spirit realm before God can fully accomplish what He desires to do to bring people out of a particular area of bondage into a new area of liberty. In realisation of this, potent prayers will be offered to break what is necessary to set us free and open doors. Therefore, I prophesy and decree that all bondage in your life is broken; all adversaries are cast out, and you will enter your open door of great opportunities. In the mighty name of Jesus Christ. Amen.

PRAYER POINTS:

1. Heavenly Father, I thank You most sincerely for Your power to defend me. Your praise shall continue to fill my mouth. In the name of Jesus.

2. I plead the blood of Jesus Christ for the cleansing of any shortcoming capable of hindering my prayers. I cover myself with the blood. In the name of Jesus.

3. Holy Ghost, rekindle Your fire in me to set my prayers on fire. In the name of Jesus.

4. Holy Ghost, arise and silence the evil cry of the wicked powers of my father's house over my destiny. In the name of Jesus.

5. O God, arise and uproot everything You have not planted into the great door, which You have opened for me. In the name of Jesus.

6. I command that which hinders me from greatness to give way now! In the name of Jesus.

7. Every satanic agent on evil assignment to poison my life through food in the dream, fall and die now! In the name of Jesus.

8. Every sickness designed to hinder my advancement, fruitfulness, and success, receive permanent termination now! In the name of Jesus.

9. Satanic cloud covering my life, scatter and clear away. In the name of Jesus.

10. Every satanic agent sitting in the driver's seat of the vehicle of my progress, get out now! In the name of Jesus.

11. LORD, by Your mighty power, chase out all adversaries from the great door, which You have opened for me. In the name of Jesus.

12. I receive extraordinary power to enter new opportunities and breakthroughs in this month's programme. In the name of Jesus.

13. Anointing to excel and prosper in the new opportunities, fall mightily upon me now. In the name of Jesus.

14. I withdraw all my benefits and blessings from the hands of the oppressors. In the name of Jesus.

15. Wonderful LORD, I thank You for answering these prayers by Your fire. In the name of Jesus.

PRAYER 18

CANCEL EVERY SEASON OF LACK AND FAMINE IN MY LIFE AND FAMILY, O LORD!

BIBLE VERSES: Job 5:20, NKJV; Psalm 33:19, NKJV

INTRODUCTION

The condition of lack and famine is such that food, water, and other things of life, even God's Word are not available or in limited supply. Generally speaking, it is a challenging situation, which affects virtually every living thing: human beings, animals, plants, forests, etc. It also affects the economic, social and/or spiritual condition of a given area. In a nutshell, it is the condition of abject poverty.

The causes of lack or famine include climatic changes on the planet earth and devastating wars in nations or regions where essential products are made. It can also include the sin of disobedience to divine laws that carry divine consequences. These situations create extreme shortages of resources, famine, destruction, and untimely death to the people in the affected area, region or the entire world.

Lack, famine, destruction, and death are never comfortable situations. They require divine intervention. Hence, believers in Christ – or better still – God's children, are expected to be aware of those things that give rise to such situations and avoid them as much as possible. Furthermore, we must obey God's Word, have absolute faith, trust and pray for God to shield or deliver believers from any dryness and continue to enjoy the supernatural abundance, care, and comfort of the Almighty God.

Because of the negative impact of lack and famine, it is important to pray against such conditions in advance or deal with them swiftly and seriously if they have a tendency to show up in our lives. I prophesy, therefore, that the LORD shall arise and cancel every challenging situation: lack, famine, destruction or death out of your life. In Jesus' mighty name. Amen.

PRAYER POINTS:

1. Mighty One of Israel, I give You glory and honour for Your wonderful work in my life and family. May Your name be praised forever. In the name of Jesus.

2. I plead the blood of Jesus for total cleansing and coverage. In the name of Jesus.

3. O God of Elijah, send down Your fire and ignite my prayers today. In the name of Jesus.

4. Powers supplying strength to problems in my life, die by fire. In the name of Jesus.

5. Fire of God, consume every object or instrument of failure and regret in my life. In Jesus' name.

6. Every source of lack, famine, destruction, and death in my life and family, dry up by the fire of God. In the name of Jesus.

7. Evil dedication flowing from my foundation, be cut off and dried up. In the name of Jesus.

8. Environmental powers assigned against my prosperity, be consumed by the fire of God. In the name of Jesus.

9. O God, arise and fight every visible and invisible battle from the dark kingdom against my life. In the name of Jesus.

10. Blood of Jesus, block every channel of poverty or demonic scarcity in my life. In the name of Jesus.

11. I withdraw my wealth and prosperity from the hands of the bound woman and her children. In the name of Jesus.

12. My head, reject satanic manipulation and untimely death. In the name of Jesus.

13. My prosperity and glory, what are you doing in the custody of the household enemies? Come out by fire and locate me. In the name of Jesus.

14. O LORD God of signs and wonders, arise and cancel every season of lack and famine in my life. In the name of Jesus.

15. Wonderful LORD, I thank You for answering these prayers by fire. In the name of Jesus.

PRAYER 19

CONFOUND MY ADVERSARIES WITH YOUR PEACE AND PROSPERITY IN MY LIFE, O LORD!

BIBLE VERSES: *Psalm 40:14, 15 (AMP).*

INTRODUCTION

Adversaries are enemies. When they are confounded, it means they are surprised, confused, and proved wrong in their actions. Adversaries will always look for every opportunity to bring their victims down, even to the pit, that is, to the point of elimination by death. But when the LORD does the confounding by using His peace and prosperity to counter-act the adversaries in the lives of their victims, it is the highest level of confusion and disgrace for them.

David, in our Bible verse, prayed to the LORD for intervention. He knew fully well that vengeance belongs to the LORD. He gave the matter to Him and his words were suggestions of the kind of intervention he would like to see. David's style of strong words in his prayers was meant to motivate us always into taking a strong stand against sin and evil.

Our desires and expectations shall be fulfilled when we pray these prayers in line with the above reality, I prophesy, therefore, that the LORD will arise and confound all your adversaries with His peace and prosperity in your life. In Jesus' mighty name. Amen.

PRAYER POINTS:

1. Most gracious God, I give You praise, honour, and adoration for Your faithfulness in my life and for all you have done for me.

2. I plead the blood of Jesus Christ and cover myself and all that belongs to me with the blood. In the name of Jesus.

3. Holy Ghost, ignite my prayers with Your fire. In the name of Jesus.

4. Foundational powers of my father's house exposing my life to the adversary, your end has come. Die by the fire of God! In the name of Jesus.

5. LORD, expose the evil agenda of the household enemies of my father's house and frustrate them. In the name of Jesus.

6. LORD, release Your judgment of death upon the satanic powers attacking the peace of God in my life and family. In the name of Jesus.

7. Holy Ghost, uproot by Your fire the seeds of envy and reproach sown into the foundation of my life. In the name of Jesus.

8. Oppressing and manipulating powers in my life, be disgraced out of my life. In the name of Jesus.

9. LORD, that which my adversaries are relying upon to boast about before me, turn it into a snare to swallow them up. In the name of Jesus.

10. LORD, destroy every gadget, which the adversaries are using to monitor my life and family. In the name of Jesus.

11. Every instrument of torment prepared by the stubborn enemies for my life and family, LORD, command it to be used against them. In the name of Jesus.

12. Whatever makes You God over all the earth, LORD, use it to confound my adversaries in their plan to frustrate my life. In the name of Jesus.

13. By Your great and unsearchable power, LORD, confuse my adversaries with Your peace and prosperity in my life and family. In the name of Jesus.

14. Ancestral idols of my father's house contending with my deliverance and salvation catch fire and die! In the name of Jesus.

15. The LORD shall cause me to rejoice in the victory He has given me over my adversaries. In the name of Jesus.

16. Gracious LORD, I thank You for answering these prayers by fire. In the name of Jesus.

PRAYER 20

BLESS AND KEEP ME, O LORD!

BIBLE VERSE: *Numbers 6:24 (NKJV)*

INTRODUCTION

"To be blessed" is to be divinely favoured and "to keep" is to be protected. When you ask God to bless and keep you, it is an important way of seeking God's divine favour and protection. These two aspects of human life are needed to ensure abundant and victorious living.

God is the Creator and Maker of all things including human beings. Thus, He is the source of all the good things in life, which He freely gives for the benefit of His people. At various times in the Scriptures, God emphasized He will bless and keep us. For example, He will, "instruct and teach us in the way we should go and guide us with His eyes" (Psalm 32:8), "order the steps of the righteous" (Psalm 37:23), "give the power to get wealth" (Deuteronomy 8:18), "never leave us or forsake us" (Hebrews 13:5) and keep in perfect peace those whose minds are stayed on Him (Isaiah 26:3) to mention a few.

In praying the following prayers, the LORD's hands shall be opened for the blessings and care to flow. I prophesy, therefore, that every obstacle and hindrance shall be dismantled and put out of the way. The year will be filled with divine favour and protection. In Jesus' mighty name. Amen.

PRAYER POINTS:

1. Our most gracious and covenant-keeping God, I worship and honour You for your wonderful works in my life and family over the years. All praises and adoration unto You. In Jesus' name.

2. Let your mercy, O LORD, swallow up all my shortcomings and soak me in the precious blood of Jesus Christ. In Jesus' name.

3. Holy Spirit, kindle your fire in me for the journey this year. In the name of Jesus.

4. O LORD, fill my life with your strength to face every challenge on my way In the name of Jesus.

5. Every satanic power assigned to block or hinder my way, be consumed by the fire of God. In the name of Jesus.

6. In my exploits, LORD, arise and disappoint all my adversaries. In the name of Jesus.

7. The LORD shall give me riches and wealth without sorrow. In the name of Jesus.

8. Anything I lay my hands on shall prosper. In the name of Jesus.

9. Wonderful LORD, instruct and teach me in all my plans, decisions, and actions. Guide me with Your eyes. In the name of Jesus.

10. O LORD, keep me as the apple of Your eyes and hide me under the shadow of Your wings. In the name of Jesus.

11. LORD, compass me with abundant blessings and peace. In the name of Jesus.

12. Anywhere I turn, I shall find the favour of God and men. In the name of Jesus.

13. For the rest of my life, O LORD, be my refuge and fortress. In the name of Jesus.

14. O LORD, make me walk with You and be perfect. In the name of Jesus.

15. LORD, I thank You for answering these prayers by fire. In the name of Jesus.

PRAYER 21

OPEN UNTO ME THE CHANNEL OF YOUR GREAT GOODNESS, O LORD

BIBLE VERSES: *Nehemiah 9:22-25*

INTRODUCTION

The "great goodness of God" simply means the "abundant blessings of God." To pray that the channel of the LORD's great goodness is opened to you is to ask that the flow of God's abundant blessings is put on a perpetual course in your life in the same way a river channel facilitates the constant flow of the river. God is the only one who "openeth and no man shutteth and shutteth and no man openeth" (Revelations 3:7). When God opens the channel of His goodness unto His children, no human, spirit, principality or power can shut it. Hallelujah!

The testimony of Nehemiah in today's Bible verses on the great goodness of God to the people of Israel is a clear demonstration of what God can do and the fulfillment of God's promises to those who believe in Him. However, believers have their part to play, that is, to ask the LORD in prayer to open up the channel of His great goodness and connect them to it. This "asking the LORD" is the main reason for these prayers. I prophesy, therefore, that every satanic cataract in your communication channel to God shall be cleared out and His great goodness flows into your life perpetually. In Jesus' mighty name. Amen.

PRAYER POINTS:

1. Gracious God, I give You praise and honour for the fact that You are the source and giver of all goodness. May Your wonderful name be glorified forever. In Jesus' name.

2. I plead the blood of Jesus Christ and cover myself and all that belongs to me with the precious blood. In the name of Jesus.

3. Holy Ghost, ignite my prayers today with Your fire. In the name of Jesus.

4. Holy Spirit, let the power the Enemy is relying on to attack Your goodness in my life be rendered impotent. In the name of Jesus.

5. LORD, let the instrument the Enemy plans to use against me be used against him. In the name of Jesus.

6. O LORD, rescue me from the valley of trouble, struggle, and defeat. Translate me into the mountain of victory, success, and peace. In the name of Jesus.

7. Let the efforts of all the stubborn pursuers in my life and family be wasted. In the name of Jesus.

8. All the information about my life in the hands of the Enemy is rendered useless. In the name of Jesus.

9. Those who become angry when they see me, O LORD, put them into perpetual sorrow and unhappiness. In the name of Jesus.

10. All the rage of the Enemy against my breakthroughs is silenced! In the name of Jesus.

11. O LORD, take out my glory from the midst of mean men and lift it up for the world to see. In the name of Jesus.

12. Every spiritual and physical cataract in the channel of the goodness of God to me is cleared out. In the name of Jesus.

13. Spirit of the Living God, cause the channel of Your great goodness to open unto me now and henceforth, flow perpetually. In the name of Jesus.

14. I shall not squander my divine opportunities and blessings. In the name of Jesus.

15. Gracious Father, I thank You for answering my prayers by Your fire. In the name of Jesus.

PRAYER 22

OPEN UNTO ME THE DOOR OF GREAT OPPORTUNITIES, O LORD!

BIBLE VERSE: John 10:9

INTRODUCTION

A door is a form of barrier at the entrance of a room or building. When opened it provides easy access. The LORD Jesus Christ in the Bible verse describes Himself as the door through which any man can enter and draw from the various benefits that have been provided by God for man. These include salvation and prosperity.

In the journey of life, every believer is expected to grow in the grace received through salvation. They are supposed to attain success in spiritual, as well as physical endeavours through the opportunities provided by the LORD. Such prayers that can facilitate success in these areas must, of necessity, include the opening of doors of opportunities by the LORD.

In Psalm 23:2, the LORD, in His caring function, leads His own sheep into green pastures and still waters – a bundle of refreshing opportunities. Also, in another place, the LORD describes Himself as "He who has the key of David, He who opens, and no one shuts, and shuts and no man opens" (Revelations 3:7, NKJV). It naturally follows that we must direct our prayers to the LORD and let Him provide the gateway for the great expectations to be fulfilled. Therefore, I prophesy that the LORD as the door Himself shall open great opportunities to you. In Jesus' mighty name. Amen.

PRAYER POINTS:

1. Everlasting Father, I give You praise, honour, and adoration for the great work You have done and are doing in my life. In the name of Jesus.

2. I soak myself and all that belongs to me in the blood of Jesus Christ. In the name of Jesus.

3. Holy Ghost, ignite my prayer with Your fire. In the name of Jesus.

4. Strongman of my father's house seeking to lock me out of my door of great opportunities, fall down and die by fire now! In the name of Jesus.

5. Spirits of stagnation, limitation, and frustration in my life, die by fire. In the name of Jesus.

6. Powers that are assigned to keep me perpetually blind to the channel of my breakthrough, die by fire. In the name of Jesus.

7. LORD, dismantle every door of brass or iron set up by the dark kingdom against my blessings. In the name of Jesus.

8. I chase out the spirit of confusion from every decision taken about the opportunities opened to me. In the name of Jesus.

9. I refuse to lock the doors of success and blessings against myself. In the name of Jesus.

10. O LORD, in Your infinitive mercies, open the door of great opportunities unto me. In the name of Jesus.

11. Lift up your heads everlasting doors and let the King of Glory come into my life. In the name of Jesus.

12. I shall never misuse the opportunities for breakthroughs already given to me by the LORD. In the name of Jesus.

13. I barricade my life from all destiny diverters. In the name of Jesus.

14. I receive the grace to remain great in the great opportunities the LORD shall give me. In the name of Jesus.

15. LORD, I thank You for answering these prayers by fire. In the name of Jesus.

PRAYER 23

MAKE YOUR FACE SHINE UPON ME, O LORD!

BIBLE VERSE: Psalm 119:135 (NKJV)

INTRODUCTION

The prayer "Make Your face shine upon me, O LORD" is an important one, which simply asks the LORD to be glad, pleased, and/or satisfied with the person making the prayer. It is for such a person to be approved of the LORD. Hence, the prayer is an excellent way for you to receive all-round blessings (protection, provision, peace, etc.) from the LORD.

The desire of the LORD is for true believers in Him to be in this excellent spiritual state. This desire was demonstrated in His instruction to Aaron through Moses in Numbers 6:25 to bless the children of Israel with this kind of blessing. However, not every believer in Christ can attain this excellent spiritual position due to:

1. inadequate knowledge of God's Word (Psalm 119:11)
2. ignorance of the Devil's devices (2 Corinthians 2:11)
3. carelessness in spiritual things (James 4:7-10)
4. faithlessness (Hebrews 11:6)
5. prayerlessness (Luke 18:1)

On the Mount of Transfiguration, the disciples of Jesus Christ heard God's voice saying, "This is my beloved Son in whom I am well pleased; hear him" (Matthew 17:5). When God saw the success recorded in producing Jesus Christ, God was delighted and then asked the world to hear Him (Jesus). Through Jesus, anyone who obeys can rise to His same level. The secret of Jesus Christ's success is His obedience to everything God told Him and consistent prayers.

In these prayers, in addition to highlighting those things that can defeat the believer, you will, like David, cry unto the LORD to translate you into that excellent status before Him. Therefore, I prophesy that every object of hindrance in your life shall be rolled away and the LORD will make His face shine upon you henceforth. In Jesus' mighty name. Amen.

PRAYER POINTS:

1. Omnipotent God, I bless Your most holy name for making me a part of this month's programme and the promised blessings. In the name of Jesus.

2. I soak myself and all that belongs to me in the precious blood of Jesus Christ. In Jesus' name.

3. I command any satanic power or force planning to hinder my prayers today to fall down and die by fire. In the name of Jesus.

4. LORD, make my voice precious in your ears today and cause my petition to receive prompt attention. In the name of Jesus.

5. Whatever legal ground or platform Satan is relying on to accuse me before You, LORD, destroy them by Your infinitive mercies and the blood of Jesus. In Jesus' name.

6. Evil champion of my father's house manipulating my destiny, receive double destruction. In the name of Jesus.

7. Every pattern of poverty and struggle in my life and family, expire by fire. In the name of Jesus.

8. LORD, whatever the Enemy has done to disorganize Your plan and promises for my life and

family, nullify it by the blood of Jesus Christ. In Jesus' name.

9. Holy Ghost fire, burn and reduce to ashes all generational powers blocking the channel of my divine blessings. In the name of Jesus.

10. Holy Ghost, chase out by Your fire all those covering up the announcement of my physical and spiritual promotion. In the name of Jesus.

11. Every seed of near-success syndrome planted in my life, die by fire. In the name of Jesus.

12. Powers of shame and disgrace assigned against my life and destiny, fall and die by fire. In the name of Jesus.

13. LORD, renew Your covenant of mercy and peace upon my life and family. In the name of Jesus.

14. By Your divine power, O LORD, plant my feet on higher ground and make Your face shine upon me. In the name of Jesus.

15. LORD, I thank You for giving me the power to ask, believe, and receive my request with thanksgiving. In the name of Jesus.

PRAYER 24

MAKE ME FRUITFUL IN EVERY GOOD WORK, O LORD!

BIBLE VERSE: Colossians 1:10

INTRODUCTION

To be "fruitful" is to be capable of producing fruit. "Every good work" is that kind of work or duty that is classified as good. To ask the LORD to make you fruitful in every good work, therefore, is a request to be full of success in the good work you do.

In our Bible verse, it is clearly stated a person who walks worthy of the LORD produces fruitfulness that is pleasing. Also, in Galatians Chapter 6, it is written that every believer is expected to "prove his own work" (Galatians 6:4) and such work has to be "good unto all men" (Galatians 6:10). It is submitted here that every good work that is done in love, righteousness, integrity, sincerity or mercy, and without doubt amounts to good work.

Of necessity, fruitfulness in every good work must result in the manifestation of God's glory in addition to the joy of doing such work. However, apostle Paul says, "I do not understand what I do; for I don't do what I would like to do, but instead I do what I hate" (Romans 7:15, GNV). Paul clearly identified one element: the flesh as a serious hindrance to doing good work. Hence, we need to cry unto the LORD to prepare us by pruning, so we can continue to be fruitful. Therefore, I prophesy that the LORD shall carry out the pruning in your life on a regular basis and make you fruitful in every good work of eternal value. In Jesus' mighty name. Amen.

PRAYER POINTS:

1. Most righteous Father, I thank You and give You praise and adoration for all You are set to do for me in these prayers.

2. O LORD, dip me in the blood of Jesus Christ and the full measure of Your mercy and grace. In the name of Jesus.

3. The LORD rebuke you spirits of hardship and wretchedness. Lose your hold upon my life and destiny. In the name of Jesus.

4. Any object of reproach and disgrace planted into my body in the dream, be flushed out by the blood of Jesus. In Jesus' name.

5. Every plan and design by the kingdom of darkness to choke up the God-given seed in my life and ministry shall not stand or come to pass. In the name of Jesus.

6. LORD, chase every devourer of my harvest out of my life and command them to be consumed by Your fire. In the name of Jesus.

7. LORD, destroy every power that is preventing me from walking worthy of You unto all pleasing. In the name of Jesus.

8. Holy Ghost fire, dismantle every satanic embargo built against my fruitfulness. In the name of Jesus.

9. Blood of Jesus, break and nullify every covenant that has tied my life to darkness or occultism. In the name of Jesus.

10. LORD, give unto me now the divine power that will direct and lead me into doing good work. In the name of Jesus.

11. Dew of heaven, fall upon my endeavours now and cause every seed sown in righteousness to produce the desired bountiful harvest. In the name of Jesus.

12. LORD, change my time and situation for the best. Make all things beautiful in my life and family. In the name of Jesus.

13. I shall continue to flourish like the palm tree and bring forth fruits even in my old age. In the name of Jesus.

14. In my Christian journey, I shall not only abound in good works, but I will also be fruitful in them. In the name of Jesus.

15. LORD, once again, I thank You for answering these prayers. In the name of Jesus.

PRAYER 25

COMPASS MY LIFE WITH YOUR SEASON OF MERCY AND FAVOUR, O LORD!

BIBLE VERSES: Ecclesiastes 3:1; Psalm 102:13

INTRODUCTION

Ecclesiastes 3:1 says in part, "To everything there is a season." God has a plan for all people; thus, He provides cycles of life with each having its work for us to do.

As believers in Christ, we are called unto a living hope of eternal and abundant life through what God has done for us in Christ Jesus. Specifically speaking, God the Father, in His great mercy chose us before we chose Him. Jesus Christ the Son died for us while we were still sinners, and the Holy Spirit brings us the benefits of salvation, which include freedom from sin, favour, and peace with God (1 Peter 1:2-3).

Although we may face many problems in the world that seem to contradict God's plan, these should not be barriers to believing in Him. Rather, they should be opportunities to discover that without God, life's problems have no lasting solutions. A life approved by God is one that does not cover sins but confesses and forsakes them (Proverbs 28:13); the person makes Jesus Christ his or her personal Saviour and LORD.

The secret to receiving blessings and peace from God is to discover, accept, and appreciate God's perfect timing. As God's Word makes it clear, the time (and season) for His mercy and favour upon you is now. It naturally follows that when this truth is discovered and understood, it is appropriated in prayer into our lives. I prophesy, therefore, that the LORD compasses your Life with His season of mercy and favour. In Jesus' mighty name. Amen.

PRAYER POINTS:

1. Merciful and gracious Father, I bless and magnify Your most holy name for all You have done and will continue to do for me through this programme. In the name of Jesus.

2. I confess that You are the Christ and LORD over my life. In the name of Jesus.

3. I plead the precious blood of Jesus and cover myself, as well as all that belongs to me with the blood. In the name of Jesus.

4. I renounce, break, and nullify every curse or covenant made against my prosperity unawares to me by my ancestors or anybody on my behalf. In the name of Jesus.

5. Holy Spirit, reveal to me any aspect of my life standing as the problem to my progress. By Your power correct me. In the name of Jesus.

6. LORD, command Your host of heaven to block the way of stubborn evil intruders in my life and family. In the name of Jesus.

7. Holy Ghost, consume all the objects of stagnation, limitation, and frustration in my environment by Your fire. In the name of Jesus.

8. Holy Ghost, chase away every enemy of God among my friends from me. In the name of Jesus.

9. Whatsoever is responsible for affliction in my life, LORD, remove it and disgrace those who are rejoicing over such affliction. In the name of Jesus.

10. Sickness and untimely death, my life is not your candidate, therefore, fall and die! In the mighty name of Jesus.

11. Powers that vow to make my journey through life fruitless, Holy Ghost thunder, shatter them to pieces. In the name of Jesus.

12. The Bible says the blessing of the LORD makes rich, and He adds no sorrow with it; therefore, I reject and shake every blessing that is not of the LORD out of my life. In Jesus' name.

13. O LORD, roll out Your season of mercy and uncommon favour for my life and family now! In the name of Jesus.

14. My Father and my God, do not allow Your gifts and blessings in my life to become the source of fleshly pride for me. In the name of Jesus.

15. LORD, I thank You for answering these prayers and for the testimonies that will follow. In the name of Jesus.

PRAYER 26

POSITION ME FOR DIVINE INCREASE, O LORD.

BIBLE VERSES: *1 Corinthians 3:7; Psalm 115:14*

INTRODUCTION

"Divine increase" is the supply of anything in excess of the normal quantity by the supernatural power of God. Therefore, being positioned for divine increase means you become eligible and ready to receive supernatural increase from God.

We all desire and long to have supernatural increase in all our ways and endeavours. Divine increase does not follow the pattern or principles of investment, which states that the return on investment increases with the increase in the amount of capital employed. Divine increase is the exclusive preserve of God (Genesis 26:1-4, 12).

As part of God's covenant with His people, divine increase comes out of God's love and grace in answer to the prayers of His children who ask Him. Hence, in praying the following prayers, you will be able to tarry before the

Almighty God and ask for this extraordinary blessings. I prophesy, therefore, that the LORD shall be gracious unto you and position you strategically for the desired increase. In Jesus' mighty name. Amen.

PRAYER POINTS:

1. Wonderful God, I bless and worship You for being there for me all the time as the source of all increase.

2. I plead the blood of Jesus Christ for cleansing and total coverage. In the name of Jesus.

3. Blood of Jesus, break and nullify every generational or ancestral curse working against my prosperity. In the name of Jesus.

4. LORD, dismantle every form of limitation put upon me by environmental powers. In the name of Jesus.

5. LORD, separate me from every evil friend and parasite seeking to decrease me. In the name of Jesus.

6. Every evil report used to hinder my promotion, Holy Ghost, burn it and its source to ashes by Your fire. In the name of Jesus.

7. I reject and chase every spirit of retrogression and set-back out of my life. In the name of Jesus.

8. I command every spirit of slavery and servitude to get out of my life. In the name of Jesus.

9. Holy Ghost, by Your fire, tear off and burn the satanic veil covering my divine vision. In the name of Jesus.

10. Holy Spirit, frustrate every satanic investment proposal designed to ruin my life. In the name of Jesus.

11. By Your mighty power, LORD, position me for divine increase and block out every enemy of my blessings. In the name of Jesus.

12. My prosperity from the north, south, east, and west, no more delay, begin to manifest in my life. In the name of Jesus

13. It is written and I declare it. The LORD shall increase me and every member of my family more and more. In the mighty name of Jesus.

14. It is written and I declare it. The LORD shall increase my greatness and comfort me on every side. In the name of Jesus.

15. LORD, I thank You for answers to these prayers and the manifold blessings received. In the name of Jesus.

PRAYER 27

SATISFY ME WITH HONEY OUT OF THE ROCK, O LORD

BIBLE VERSES: *Psalm 81:16; Deuteronomy 32:13*

INTRODUCTION

"Honey" is the substance made by bees (a type of wild insect) from sweet fluids collected from plants, while "rock" is the hard part of the earth's soil or a large stone. Honey is good and very rich in value and usefulness. However, the process of getting honey from its source (honeycomb) is very difficult and dangerous. To get honey out of the rock, naturally, is an impossible task because honey and rock are mutually exclusive (practically unrelated components).

Spiritually, honey can represent all the good, precious, and delicious things of life the LORD uses to nourish His creatures. Because it is of the Spirit, its source and flow can only be from God. To satisfy someone with honey out of the rock can only be a spiritual request. It is a desire expressed in prayer for God to supernaturally care for us.

The poverty of those who know not God or who rebel against Him comes from losing the privilege of drawing from those God-given delicious things of life.

In our daily needs as God's children, it is absolutely necessary for us to be cared for by our heavenly Father, God who alone can supply all our needs both spiritually and physically, however difficult such need may be. The Bible says, "I am the LORD your God who brought you out of the land of Egypt; Open your mouth wide, and I will fill it" (Psalm 81:10, NKJV). Knowing God as omnipotent and unlimited in caring for His creatures, the Bible says further, "You open Your hand and satisfy the desire of every living thing" (Psalm 145:16, NKJV). It is appropriate to cry unto God to receive the fulfillment of His promises. Therefore, I prophesy that the LORD shall hear, answer, and load you daily with all the good, precious, and delicious things of life. In Jesus' mighty name. Amen.

PRAYER POINTS:

1. LORD God Almighty, I lift You and Your name higher above any other name and power. Be exalted forever. In the name of Jesus.

2. I plead the blood of Jesus Christ for cleansing and total coverage. In the name of Jesus.

3. Holy Ghost fire, consume every generational power assigned against God's favour in my life. In the name of Jesus.

4. Ancestral power mocking my God-given destiny, be disgraced by the blood of Jesus. In the name of Jesus.

5. Every satanic agitation over my life, be frustrated. In the name of Jesus.

6. Stretch Your mighty hands, O LORD, and draw me out of every river of adversity. In the name of Jesus.

7. As I open my mouth wide according to Your Word, O LORD, fill it with your extraordinary power and authority. In the name of Jesus.

8. As I hearken unto Your Word now, O LORD, satisfy me with honey out of the rock. In the name of Jesus.

9. Dear LORD, satisfy me abundantly with Your goodness and the fatness of Your house. Make me drink from the river of Your pleasure. In the name of Jesus.

10. O LORD, make me draw water with joy out of the wells of Your salvation from generation to generation. In the name of Jesus.

11. As I open my life wide unto You, O LORD, fill it with Your glory and comfort. In the name of Jesus.

12. Because the LORD of hosts is with me and the God of Jacob is my refuge, I remain confident in His care. In the name of Jesus.

13. Because the eternal God is my refuge, His everlasting arms are underneath me. Therefore, I shall not be swept away by the storms of life. In the name of Jesus.

14. The LORD shall make me ride on the higher places of the earth and eat of the increase of the field. In the name of Jesus.

15. LORD, I thank You for answering these prayers by Your fire. In the name of Jesus.

PRAYER 28

MAKE ME DRINK OF THE RIVER OF THY PLEASURE, O LORD

BIBLE VERSE: Psalm 36:8

INTRODUCTION

To drink of the river of God's pleasures, spiritually, is to have the goodness (health, wealth, protection, comfort, and deliverance) promised by God in His Word. God is the source of all goodness, which is also the heritage of His children.

Right from the beginning of the world, God set the abundance of His goodness to mankind in place by His words. "And God blessed them and God said unto them, 'Be fruitful, and multiply, and replenish the earth, and subdue it, and have dominion over the fish of the sea, and over the fowl of the air, and over every living thing that moveth upon the earth'" (Genesis 1:28).

Even though this glorious estate was lost by the first human beings through sin, the dominion was eventually returned through the atonement of the blood of our LORD Jesus

Christ. Henceforth, those who are identified with Jesus Christ as children of God are expected to walk with Him in righteousness and be close to Him in prayers. By so doing, they can draw from the goodness of the returned dominion.

In praying these prayers, we must cry unto God for the aspects of our inheritance that have still not been returned to us. Hence, I prophesy that every impediment to the goodness of God in your life shall be taken out of the way and you shall drink of the river of God's pleasure forever. In Jesus' mighty name. Amen.

PRAYER POINTS:

1. Heavenly Father, I bless Your most holy name for the victory and blessing, which You will give to me through these prayers today.

2. I plead the blood of Jesus Christ for cleansing and total coverage. In the name of Jesus.

3. O God, arise and frustrate every satanic agitation over my prayers today. In the name of Jesus.

4. LORD, visit the foundation of my life and correct every manipulation of my star at birth by household witchcraft. In the name of Jesus.

5. Every form of opposition or obstacle in my way of success and comfort, be dismantled by the fire of God. In the name of Jesus.

6. LORD, disgrace all the enemies of Your goodness in my life. In the name of Jesus.

7. As my Good Shepherd, O LORD, make me lie down in green pastures and lead me beside the still waters. In the name of Jesus.

8. LORD, set Your ambushes against the enemies of my peace and comfort. In the name of Jesus.

9. Make me walk before You in righteousness, O LORD, and draw me close to You. In the name of Jesus.

10. My Father and my God, make me drink of the river of Your goodness. In the name of Jesus.

11. The goodness and mercy of God shall be my portion in the land of the living. In the name of Jesus.

12. LORD, translate my life into the level that will bring glory and honour to Your most holy name. In the name of Jesus.

13. O LORD, the river if Your pleasure shall flow into my life forever. In the name of Jesus.

14. With Your mighty hand of righteousness, O LORD, uphold me to the end. In the name of Jesus.

15. LORD, I thank You for answers to my prayers and the blessings that will follow. In the name of Jesus.

PRAYER 29

WATER MY DRY LAND, O LORD

BIBLE VERSES: Isaiah 41:17 – 18

INTRODUCTION

Water is an important element in the life-sustaining components provided by God for all living beings. Water is valuable and unique in that it is useful in virtually every sphere of human life and has no direct substitute. Water is expected to be available everywhere to provide necessary sustenance for all living beings. A place where water cannot be found is by nature "dry." It is referred to as "dry land."

When "dry land" is applied to a spiritual situation of any person or place, it clearly indicates a very unpleasant condition: extreme poverty, serious lack of comfort or the absence of good prospects, etc. The nature of dry land and its difficult situation makes it detestable.

As it is clearly stated in the Bible verses, the solution to reviving spiritually dry land remains divine. In other words, only God can do it (Isaiah 44:18). Hence, the following prayers are aimed at seeking divine intervention in turning every unpleasant situation around for good through the power and greatness of God. Therefore, I prophesy that ever dry land in your life shall be turned into a spring of blessings. In the mighty name of Jesus.

PRAYER POINTS:

1. Father LORD, I give You praise, honour, and adoration for what You are going to do in my life today.

2. I plead the blood of Jesus Christ for cleansing and total coverage. In the name of Jesus.

3. LORD, empower me with Your authority for definite success in my prayers now. In the name of Jesus.

4. By Your authority, O LORD, recreate Your picture for my life that is damaged by sin and the Devil. In the name of Jesus.

5. LORD, give me deep knowledge of my environment and lead me to take over. In the name of Jesus.

6. Blood of Jesus, break and nullify every ancestral curse upon my environment. In the name of Jesus.

7. Holy Ghost fire, dismantle every satanic embargo on my life and destiny. In the name of Jesus.

8. Every form of barrenness in my life as a result of barrenness in the land I am standing on, be uprooted by the fire of God. In the name of Jesus.

9. LORD, destroy every instrument of the wicked assigned against my prosperity by Your fire. In the name of Jesus.

10. As I cry unto You now, O LORD, turn every dryness in the land I am standing on into springs of water. In the name of Jesus.

11. LORD, command all the good things in my life and destiny that have died to receive life now! In the name of Jesus.

12. LORD, guide me into fulfilling Your purpose for my life henceforth. In the name of Jesus.

13. I shall flourish like the palm tree and grow like the cedar of Lebanon. In the name of Jesus.

14. My horn shall be exalted like that of a unicorn, and I shall be anointed with fresh oil. In the name of Jesus.

15. LORD, I thank You for answering these prayers and the testimonies that will follow. In the name of Jesus.

PRAYER 30

PUT A NEW SONG INTO TO MOUTH

BIBLE VERSES: Psalm 40:1–3

INTRODUCTION

When we offer the prayer "Put a new song into my mouth, O LORD," we are asking the LORD to change the current story of our lives into a new one. In other words, the LORD is the one who will do a new thing in our lives.

In the Bible verses, David, in his testimony, has shown that the process, which leads to singing a new song involves us crying unto God to intervene in our lives. Such intervention comes in the form of deliverance from situations that cause stagnation, limitation or embargo. We must wait patiently for His action. The beauty of the process is the readiness of God to do a new thing in the lives of His children. God said, "Behold, I will do a new thing: now it shall spring forth; shall ye not know it?" (Isaiah 43:19).

The primary purpose of the Devil's attack on the children of God is to prevent them from enjoying the freedom they have in Jesus Christ. The Devil, through his tricks, will cause anyone, even believers, to sin. By his manipulation, he will lead the unsuspecting into his bondage. While in bondage, the person will continue to move in circles and his/her life is characterized by stagnation. The Bible enjoins believers to be mindful of the devices of the Devil: "Lest Satan should get an advantage of us for we are not ignorant of his devices" (2 Corinthians 2:11).

As children of God, we must learn to clean our lives thoroughly and stand pure and holy before the holy God. Sin, when recognized, should be dealt with promptly. Potent prayers must be offered to destroy all the satanic operations and bondage in our lives that may be influenced by sin. Hence, the following prayers will provide the avenue to cry unto God for our stories to change for the better, so we can sing a new song. God is waiting to hear you (Jeremiah 29:12, 13). I prophesy, therefore, that every power of stagnation and limitation in your life shall be destroyed. The LORD shall do a new thing in your life and put a new song into your mouth. In Jesus' mighty name. Amen.

PRAYER POINTS:

1. LORD, I bless Your most holy name for what You have been doing in my life.

2. I soak myself and all that belongs to me into the precious blood of Jesus Christ. In Jesus' name.

3. Holy Ghost, turn me into Your fire for this prayer assignment. In the name of Jesus.

4. Holy Ghost, paralyze and disgrace every strongman and gatekeeper of satanic bondage harassing my life. In the name of Jesus.

5. Household witchcraft assigned against the peace and prosperity of my life, receive double destruction by the Holy Ghost. In the name of Jesus.

6. Every satanic embargo, roadblock or checkpoint built against my life and destiny, be dismantled by the fire of God. In the name of Jesus.

7. Spirits of stagnation, limitation, and frustration in my life, die by the fire of God. In the name of Jesus.

8. By Your mighty hands, O LORD, cast my feet out of the horrible pit of life. In the name of Jesus.

9. Every snare of the Enemy set down for me, be consumed by the fire of God. In the name of Jesus.

10. LORD, frustrate every plan and decision of the dark kingdom to kill my miracles. In the name of Jesus.

11. LORD, according to Your Word, send all my adversaries into the captivity they designed for me. In the name of Jesus.

12. I receive the power and strength to stand and operate on the solid rock henceforth. In the name of Jesus.

13. I receive the power and grace from the LORD to sing new songs. In the name of Jesus.

14. My testimony of joy and rejoicing shall not disappear. In the name of Jesus.

15. LORD, I thank You for Your answer and mighty deliverance. In the name of Jesus.

PRAYER 31

DISGRACE EVERY ENEMY OF MY DIVINE COMFORT, O LORD!

BIBLE VERSE: 2 Thessalonians 1:6,7, CEV

INTRODUCTION

Simply stated, "divine comfort" is the all-round peace that comes from God upon all His children. It is a state of complete freedom from oppression, suffering or trouble. It is not momentary as the earthly comfort is but long-lasting. To ask God to disgrace every enemy of our divine comfort is to seek God's intervention in the battle of the enemies against our God-given peace.

Satan, the Devil and accuser of the brethren, working through his demons (falling angels) and human agents are the enemies of God's children. "But pity the earth and the sea, because the devil was thrown down to the earth. He knows his time is short, and he is very angry" (Revelations 12:12, CEV). Right from the book of Genesis and spanning through the Bible to the book of Revelation, the appearance of the Devil on the scene reveals him and his agents as "deceivers," "troublers" and/or "destroyers" – names and functions that seek to put their victims into trouble or discomfort.

It is clear that Jesus Christ had already defeated Satan and put his kingdom into disarray. However, anywhere these enemies surface to vent their wrath, the power of God must be sought to deal with them for the peace of God to reign. Hence, these prayers are determined to do this. Therefore, I prophesy that the Almighty God will fight for you and all the enemies of your divine comfort shall be disgraced. In Jesus' mighty name. Amen.

PRAYER POINTS:

1. LORD God omnipotent who reigneth, I worship and adore You for what You are and for all You have done in my life through this programme. May Your most holy name be praised forever. In the name of Jesus.

2. I plead the blood of Jesus Christ for total cleansing and coverage. In the name of Jesus.

3. Spirit of religion in the foundation of my life, which is troubling my life, be uprooted and die by the fire of God. In the name of Jesus.

4. Every seed of suffering, trouble or discomfort sown into my life, be uprooted by the fire of God. In the name of Jesus.

5. Every arrow of suffering, trouble or discomfort fired into my life, come out and return to the senders. In the name of Jesus.

6. Every covenant and record of sorrow and discomfort made on my behalf in the dark kingdom, break and burn to ashes. In the name of Jesus.

7. LORD, by Your mighty power, expose every satanic agenda of discomfort for my life and frustrate it. In the name of Jesus.

8. LORD, put every miserable comforter in my life into permanent silence. In the name of Jesus.

9. O LORD, my strength, pull me out of the net the Enemy laid privately for me. In the name of Jesus.

10. LORD, decree into my life now all the instruments of Your comfort such as obedience, good health, wealth, all-round prosperity, wisdom, knowledge, and understanding. In the name of Jesus.

11. LORD, any discomfort that comes into my life due to Your chastening, be merciful and cancel it now. In the name of Jesus.

12. LORD, command Your peace, which passes all understanding, to keep and rule my heart, as well as my mind through Christ Jesus.

13. From now on and the rest of my life, I shall no longer suffer, be in sorrow or fret about anything whatsoever. In the name of Jesus.

14. From now, LORD, hide me in the secret of Your presence. In the name of Jesus.

15. LORD, I thank You for answering these prayers by fire. In the name of Jesus.

PRAYER 32

EXTEND UNTO ME YOUR PEACE AND COMFORT, O LORD!

BIBLE VERSES: (Isaiah 66:12-14).

INTRODUCTION

Peace and comfort are part of the heritage of the saints of God (the faithful and righteous ones).

The covenant of peace and comfort was part of the original plan of God in the creation of heaven and the earth. However, the covenant was broken and the peace and comfort lost through the sin of the first man. Since the curse of man and loss of the original glory, mankind continued to grope under the fear of virtually everything. But the eternal plan of God for righteousness is to put an end to sin, reconcile mankind, and make all things new.

Although we live in a horrible and most unsecured world at the present time, it is absolutely necessary as saints (believers) to appropriate God's Word through the prophet Isaiah in our Bible verses of today. That way, we will live through the privilege of prayers and His divine grace to answer.

If peace and comfort are part of the rich reward God will give to His faithful people, it is appropriate for us, in these prayers, to deal with the enemies of our peace and comfort. I prophesy, therefore, that every contender of your peace and comfort shall be disgraced; your peace shall flow like a river. Your heart and bones shall flourish like a herb. In Jesus' mighty name. Amen.

PRAYER POINTS:

1. Merciful and compassionate God, I give praise and honour to Your most holy name for the blessings received so far through this programme. In the name of Jesus.

2. I plead the blood of Jesus Christ and cover myself, as well as all that belongs to me with the blood. In the name of Jesus.

3. LORD, frustrate any form of satanic invasion in my life and destiny. In the name of Jesus.

4. I break all curses issued to me by witchcraft power and command the effects to return to the sender. In the name of Jesus.

5. Spirits of fear, instability, and untimely death, I bind you and command you consumed out of my life by fire. In the name of Jesus.

6. I barricade my mind against the attacks of the Devil and his agents. In the name of Jesus.

7. In this unsecured world, LORD, build Your wall of fire round about me and my family. In the name of Jesus.

8. LORD, disgrace all the enemies of my peace. Send them into the captivity they have prepared for me. In the name of Jesus.

9. LORD, renew Your covenant of peace and comfort for my life and family. In the name of Jesus.

10. Let my bones flourish like an herb, O LORD. In the name of Jesus.

11. LORD, make every member of my family and me prosper in good health. In the name of Jesus.

12. LORD, increase Your greatness in me and comfort my family and me on every side. In the name of Jesus.

13. LORD, renew Your covenant of long life and prosperity for my life and family. In the name of Jesus.

14. Your agenda for my life and ministry shall not be aborted. In the name of Jesus.

15. Wonderful LORD, I thank You for answering these prayers by Your fire. In the name of Jesus.

DESTINY SHAPING PRAYERS

PRAYER 33

BRING ME UNTO MY DESIRED HAVEN, O LORD

BIBLE VERSES: Psalm 107:29 – 30

INTRODUCTION

God is the Creator of heaven and earth and the keeper of His people (Psalm 121:4, 5). God's people are not alive by power or might but by the Spirit and grace of God (Zechariah 4:6; Proverbs 3:22, 23). The LORD is in control of the affairs of His people at all times. He cares and sustains them in their daily challenges, desires, and actions making sure they enjoy His company and services as the Shepherd (Psalm 23:1).

The people of Israel in the wilderness on their way to the Promised Land had the LORD in the same way but in many respects, they provoked Him through acts of disobedience. However, whenever they sinned, returned to the LORD in repentance, and cried to Him, He answered, forgave them and eventually brought them unto their desired haven (Psalm 107:29).

To some people, godly dreams, goals, and aspirations may not in any way be close to fulfillment, but the Word of the LORD says, "Though they tarry, wait for it, because it will surely come, it will not tarry" (Habakkuk 2:3). Therefore, if the delay is due to any act of disobedience to God's instructions, repent and cry unto the LORD to bring you unto your desired haven. I prophesy by the authority of heaven that the LORD shall hasten His Word to perform it. In Jesus' mighty name. Amen.

PRAYER POINTS:

1. Most powerful and gracious God, I give You honour and glory for Your wonderful daily benefits to me. May Your most holy name be exalted forever. In the name of Jesus.

2. I plead the precious blood of Jesus Christ and cover myself with the blood. In the name of Jesus.

3. Holy Ghost, purify me and ignite my prayers today with Your fire. In the name of Jesus.

4. Powers of my father's house assigned to frustrate my good dreams, goals, and aspirations in life, die by the fire of God. In the name of Jesus.

5. Blood of Jesus, break and dismantle whatsoever has been done by ancestral powers to hinder my divine prosperity and comfort. In the name of Jesus.

6. Every seed of near-success syndrome planted into my life from birth by household enemies, be uprooted by the fire of God. In the name of Jesus.

7. LORD, destroy every object of reproach in my life. In the name of Jesus.

8. Holy Ghost, disarm and disgrace anyone who is boasting of evil powers to harm me. In the name of Jesus.

9. I command every dream of oppression in my life to vanish forever. In the name of Jesus.

10. Every satanic beast harassing my harvest, be slaughtered by the sword of fire. In the name of Jesus.

11. Holy Ghost, unseat all those sitting on my seat of success and victory now. In the name of Jesus.

12. I shall never be disappointed or put to shame in all my requests to God and men for my life. In the name of Jesus.

13. All those planning and waiting for my downfall to mock me shall be disappointed. They shall be witnesses to my celebrations of success soon. In the name of Jesus.

14. God's plan to bring me to my desired haven at my point of need shall not be aborted. In the name of Jesus.

15. Wonderful LORD, I thank You for answers to these prayers and the miracles that will follow. In the name of Jesus.

PRAYER 34

PLANT MY FEET ON HIGHER GROUND, O LORD

BIBLE VERSE: Esther 10:3

INTRODUCTION

When we pray "Plant my feet on higher ground, O LORD," we are asking the LORD to promote us from our present level of attainment – be it physical or spiritual – to a higher level and to sustain us there.

It is quite common for people's lives to be stagnated, that is, be in one place perpetually or move in circles from one point to another and back to the first point. More often, these situations are due to many factors, which include demonic manipulations or various forms of wickedness.

Like the story of Mordecai in the book of Esther, God has good thoughts and plans for His children. Whichever position we find ourselves in (low or high), God can change the bad for good, good for better and better for the best by His unlimited power. Before He does this, He will deal with every obstacle on the way because He is interested in what such a person is set to accomplish for Him in the higher position. However, God expects all His children to love, obey, and trust Him. Our faith in Him must be absolute. We must wait on Him in prayer for the purpose to be fulfilled.

In line with God's plan to deliver and transform lives, it is intended through these potent prayers that you are divinely promoted. Therefore, I prophesy that every chain, which holds you down in the valley shall be broken and your feet planted firmly on higher and solid ground. In Jesus' mighty name. Amen.

PRAYER POINTS:

1. LORD God Almighty, I worship and bless Your most holy name for your grace, power, and providence in my life.

2. I soak myself and all that belongs to me in the blood of Jesus. In the name of Jesus.

3. Blood of Jesus, purge every form of unrighteousness in me and make me free. In the name of Jesus.

4. Holy Ghost, turn me into Your fire to make me untouchable and unquenchable. In the name of Jesus.

5. O God, arise on my behalf today and scatter every conspiracy of dark forces assigned against my prayers. In the name of Jesus.

6. Every spirit of Haman working against my mounting into God's destiny for my life, be consumed by the fire of God. In the name of Jesus.

7. Holy Ghost fire, dismantle all the satanic cobweb on my life and destiny. In the name of Jesus.

8. O LORD, my God, frustrate every token of the liars and evil counsellors in my life. In the name of Jesus.

9. LORD, sow Your seeds of goodness and greatness into my life. In the name of Jesus.

10. My Father and my God, plant my feet on higher and solid ground now! In the name of Jesus.

11. O LORD, with all that makes You God, promote me beyond my wildest imagination. In Jesus' name.

12. Whatsoever character qualities have helped me move up shall not bring me down again. In the name of Jesus.

13. In the position of greatness prepared for me, LORD, make me a blessing to my generation. In the name of Jesus.

14. From now, I shall no more be stagnated or move in circles. I shall continue to make progress. In the name of Jesus.

15. LORD, I thank You for promptly answering these prayers and for the divine promotion. In the name of Jesus.

PRAYER 35

MAKE ME A GOOD STEWARD OF YOUR MANIFOLD GRACE, O LORD!

BIBLE VERSES: *1 Peter 4:10, 11 (NKJV)*

INTRODUCTION

Grace is defined as God's free and unmerited favour. That is, what God gives freely even when we do not deserve it. When this free gift of God becomes many and encompassing, it is referred to as "manifold." The grace of God in the life of man has the capacity of manifesting the glory of God. Thus, when the grace becomes manifold in the life of a steward (one who manages), it is capable of manifesting the exceeding glory of God.

John 3:16 says, "For God so loved the world that He gave His only begotten Son, that whoever believes in Him should not perish but have everlasting life." It clearly explains that the purpose of the New Testament and atonement in the blood of Jesus Christ was and still remains purely an act of God's grace. The work of Jesus Christ on the earth was to redeem and reconcile humanity to God by offering Himself as the sacrifice for the sins of the whole world. In doing this, Jesus Christ made as many as believe in Him and receive His grace the sons and daughters of God. The manifold grace of God was upon Jesus Christ for this assignment. No wonder the exceeding glory of God was manifested in Him.

As believers in Jesus Christ, we have received God's grace and become sons and daughters of God. We also have gifts bestowed on us by the LORD, which we are to use for various assignments for Him. These include extending the love of God to others, ministering to them, and reconciling them unto God, among others, thereby expanding the scope of sons and daughters of God. These assignments become easy and possible when we ask and receive God's manifold grace from Him. Thus, in praying these prayers, we receive and become good stewards of God's manifold grace. I prophesy, therefore, that every embargo or hindrance standing in your way shall be dismantled, and the excellence of God's manifold grace will be manifested in you. In Jesus' mighty name. Amen.

PRAYER POINTS:

1. Great Redeemer, I bless and magnify Your most holy name for the great work You are doing in my life. Receive glory, honour, and praise forever. In the name of Jesus.

2. I plead the blood of Jesus and soak myself, as well as everything that belongs to me in the blood. In the name of Jesus.

3. Every veil of darkness blocking my vision to provide room for the satanic invasion in my life, Holy Ghost, tear it off now. In the name of Jesus.

4. Every embargo of the Enemy built against my success, be dismantled by the fire of God. In the name of Jesus.

5. Properties of the dark kingdom planted in my life to destroy my ministry, catch fire and burn to ashes. In the name of Jesus.

6. Every anti-progress gadget connected to my ministerial agenda, break up and scatter. In the name of Jesus.

7. Satanic manipulation programmed into my life in the dream, be nullified by the blood of Jesus. In Jesus' name.

8. Whatever the Enemy has done to disorganize Your plan for my life, LORD, cancel it by Your blood. In the name of Jesus.

9. By all that makes You God, make me a good steward of Your manifold grace and truth. In the name of Jesus.

10. All my prosperity, blessings, and breakthroughs being held up in satanic strongholds, LORD, command their release to me by Your fire. In the name of Jesus.

11. Anti-testimony altar built against my life and destiny, be dismantled by fire. In the name of Jesus.

12. Spirit of the living God, fill my life with Your wisdom to succeed and excel in my divine assignments. In the name of Jesus.

13. I shall manifest the exceeding glory of God in the ministry of the manifold grace of God upon my life. In the name of Jesus.

14. I shall run my Christian race well and finish my course with joy. In the name of Jesus.

15. LORD, I thank You for answering these prayers by fire. In the name of Jesus.

PRAYER 36

MAKE MY LIFE YOUR TESTIMONY, O LORD

BIBLE VERSES: Genesis 18:18, 19

INTRODUCTION

A "testimony" is a declaration or supporting evidence in any situation. A "good testimony" is that declaration or evidence, which is positive and desirable. For the LORD to make your life a good testimony is for you to be approved of the LORD. Moreover, it is for your life to become a worthy example of God's desired pattern.

From our Bible verses, we can see God's approval of Abraham's life at that time. We also see what He seeks to accomplish through the testimony, that is, to put Abraham forward as an acceptable pattern of life for the human race. People like Job and David received God's testimony at one time or another. In the New Testament, God was not without such testimony. About Jesus Christ, it is written, "And suddenly a voice came out of the cloud, saying, 'This is My beloved Son, in whom I am well pleased. Hear

Him!'"(Matthew 17:5, NKJV). This testimony about Jesus Christ stands as a pattern we should follow to attain the life of the Son of God.

God is willing and anxiously waiting to give the same testimony in respect of His children, those who have received His Son, Jesus Christ, and believe in His name (John 1:12). They have accepted Jesus Christ as their LORD and Saviour and are born again (John 3:3). However, the lives of God's children that covet His testimony must be characterized by moral purity, patience, and peacefulness, so they can "shine as lights" in this dark and depraved world. A transformed life is an effective witness (testimony) to the power of God's Word.

In light of the foregoing, it is considered that through the following prayers, the LORD will deal with our shortcomings and mould our lives into His good testimony. Therefore, I prophesy that every anti-testimony in your life shall be consumed by the fire of God. He shall clothe you with the garment of His righteousness and love, for you to "shine as light." In Jesus' name. Your life shall be approved of Him and His testimony of you shall appear. In Jesus' mighty name. Amen.

PRAYER POINTS:

1. Gracious Father, I bless Your holy name for the abundance of grace bestowed upon me and Your unfailing power to answer prayers.

2. I plead the blood of Jesus Christ for cleansing and total coverage. In the name of Jesus.

3. Fire of the Holy Ghost, purify and incubate me for effectiveness in these prayers. In the name of Jesus.

4. Every evil flow of unrighteousness, impurity or idolatry from my foundation, I command you to dry up. In the name of Jesus.

5. LORD, break every generic barrier in me and move me into Your destiny for my life. In Jesus' name.

6. Every anti-testimony power of my father's house assigned against my life, be consumed by the fire of God. In the name of Jesus.

7. Altar of darkness working against the testimony of God in my life, be dismantled. In the name of Jesus.

8. Every object of distraction in my Christian journey, be consumed by the fire of God. In the name of Jesus.

9. LORD, frustrate every satanic agitation over my life and destiny. In the name of Jesus.

10. Spirits of obedience and the fear of the LORD, fill me to the fullest. In the name of Jesus.

11. LORD, let me walk with You in love and faithfulness. In the name of Jesus.

12. LORD, change the story of my life into the glory of Your kingdom. In the name of Jesus.

13. Your counsels and instructions shall continue to be my delight, O LORD. In the name of Jesus.

14. The LORD shall make me into a mighty and formidable instrument in His vineyard. In the name of Jesus.

15. Wonderful LORD, I thank You for answers to my prayers and the testimony that will follow. In the name of Jesus.

PRAYER 37

REMEMBER ME, O LORD

BIBLE VERSES: Esther 6:1 – 11

INTRODUCTION

The word "remember" can be explained as "to bring to mind" or "keep a thing in mind and recall it at will." When we pray for God to remember us, it simply means asking Him to bring our case, matter, situation or needs to His mind with a view of acting upon them.

The Bible tells us that human beings can even forget their children, but God cannot forget His promises to His children (Isaiah 49:15). When we feel God has forgotten us, our iniquities often draw us away from Him (Isaiah 59:1-2). Our insensitivities to God's Word, plans, and ways lead us to that conclusion. The truth is God has a set time to act on all His promises (Psalm 102:13).

To pray that God remembers us and for us to receive positive responses, we must clean up our lives and by His Spirit, trust and obey Him. Through our prayers, we can position ourselves for the desired miracles. I prophesy, therefore, that God will not fail you, but He will remember you. In Jesus' mighty name. Amen.

PRAYER POINTS:

1. Faithful and marvelous Father, I bless and honour You because You are the unchangeable changer.

2. I plead the blood of Jesus for cleansing and total coverage. In the name of Jesus.

3. Every conspiracy of the dark kingdom against my prayers today, scatter by the fire of God. In Jesus' name.

4. Generational power keeping the record of my blessings, surrender it and be destroyed by the fire of God. In the name of Jesus.

5. Ancestral record of failure containing my name, be roasted by fire. In the name of Jesus.

6. Any spirit of stagnation, limitation, frustration or confusion in my life, be destroyed by the fire of God. In the name of Jesus.

7. Holy Ghost fire, consume every spirit of dryness or barrenness operating in my environment. In the name of Jesus.

8. All those sitting on my letter of physical and spiritual promotion, be unseated, and surrender it now. In the name of Jesus.

9. Blood of Jesus, cancel all that has been done or is being done in the kingdom of darkness to frustrate my life. In the name of Jesus.

10. Open Your book of remembrance for me today and honour me. In the name of Jesus.

11. LORD, open my eyes to see my well of blessings. In the name of Jesus.

12. Arrows of sickness, infirmity, and untimely death fired into my life in the dream, come out and go back to your sender. In the name of Jesus.

13. By Your great power, take me from where I am now to where You want me to be. In the name of Jesus.

14. I shall possess my possession and eat the fruit of my labour. In the name of Jesus.

15. LORD, I thank You for Your prompt answer to my prayers. In the name of Jesus.

PRAYER 38

LIFT MY HEAD HIGH ABOVE THE REACH OF MAN, O LORD!

BIBLE VERSE: Psalm 27:6a

INTRODUCTION

The natural stature of a man may be short or tall, small or big in line with the endowment of God for him. For the head of a man to be lifted high above means he is raised to the height that is no longer normal. When the LORD lifts a person high above the reach of man, which is possible only in the spiritual realm, such a person is supernaturally raised in power and placed at an advantaged level.

For most of his life, David, the man after God's heart, was encompassed by troubles ranging from Goliath to Saul and those who came to him in his capacity as the king of Israel. Although he was not initially a soldier in the regular army of Israel, he fought Goliath in the LORD's power and prevailed. He escaped the assassination plots of King Saul and for the forty years of his reign as the king of Israel, he fought many battles and lost none. He was victorious because the LORD empowered him and gave him the advantage over all his enemies. The testimony of his victories is clearly captured in Psalm 18. Therefore, he was confident in his confession in the Bible verse.

As believers in Christ, we have our share of the troubles of life brought about by Satan and his human agents operating from the kingdom of darkness. Like David, we ought also to come to the point of the same confession. Hence, we must pray asking the LORD to do what He did in David. Therefore, I prophesy that the LORD shall fight your battles and lift your head high above the reach of any man. In Jesus' mighty name. Amen.

PRAYER POINTS:

1. My Father and my God, I thank You most sincerely for Your love and providence in my life.

2. I plead the precious blood of Jesus and soak myself, as well as all that belongs to me in the blood. In the name of Jesus.

3. O God, arise in Your power and fight my battles today. In the name of Jesus.

4. Holy Spirit, make all my prayers today command divine attention. In the name of Jesus.

5. Satanic chains on my hands and legs, break now! In the name of Jesus.

6. O LORD, uproot from my life evil things that are against my advancement. In the name of Jesus.

7. Every sickness assigned to pull my advancement down, receive permanent termination now. In the name of Jesus.

8. Fountain of discomfort in my life, dry up now. In the name of Jesus.

9. Power of witchcraft holding my blessings in bondage, receive the fire of God and release them. In the name of Jesus.

10. Every invisible hand working evil in my life, wither now and be burnt to ashes. In Jesus' name.

11. O LORD, lift my head high above the reach of my enemies. In the name of Jesus.

12. LORD, convert my point of ridicule to a source of uncommon miracle. In the name of Jesus.

13. LORD, turn me into an untouchable coal of fire. In the name of Jesus.

14. My life, begin to experience divine acceleration unto my mountain of prosperity. In the name of Jesus.

15. My LORD and my God, thank You for answering these prayers by Your fire. In the name of Jesus.

PRAYER 39

BRING OUT THE STAR IN ME AND CAUSE IT TO SHINE BRIGHTLY, O LORD!

BIBLE VERSE: Daniel 6:1-3

INTRODUCTION

The "star" in you is what makes you stand out in honour and in your chosen assignment, endeavour or calling making others notice you. Therefore, to pray for the LORD to bring out the star in you is to ask for divine grace to be successful and recognized in your chosen profession.

The stars are special among God's creation; each of them glows radiantly to distinguish them from other lights. In the same way, every human being is endowed by God with talent(s) or gift(s) that make each person stand out from the others. Since the tragedy of destiny recorded in Genesis Chapter 3 when the glory departed, human beings have had to seriously struggle to excel in real life. With the work of our LORD Jesus Christ on the cross and His resurrection, the attainment of excellence in life clearly becomes a matter of God's grace.

Daniel was a slave in Babylon but through the divine grace of God, he was favoured by the king to become the first among the three administrators of the kingdom. The secret of Daniel's recognition and promotion was his consecration and prayers. Believers in Christ are those who have received God's grace of salvation. Like Daniel, they can draw from the grace of God for them to "stand out" and be "recognized" as stars. Hence, we are to reach out to God with the following prayers for Him to bring out the best in us as recognition and testimony of His power and grace. I prophesy, therefore, that every embargo on or blockage of your star will be dismantled. The LORD shall bring out the star in you and cause it to shine brightly for recognition and promotion. In Jesus' mighty name. Amen.

PRAYER POINTS:

1. Gracious and everlasting God, I thank You for Your faithfulness in my life. May Your most holy name be praised forever.

2. I plead the blood of Jesus Christ for cleansing and coverage. In the name of Jesus.

3. Holy Ghost Fire, fall on me now and turn me into Your fire. In the name of Jesus.

4. Witchcraft power of my father's house contending with my life and destiny, die by fire. In the name of Jesus.

5. Every satanic veil of darkness or stubble covering my star, be torn off and consumed by the fire of God. In the name of Jesus.

6. Stretch Your hands into the foundation of my life, O LORD, and repair all the damage done to my destiny and star. In the name of Jesus.

7. All manipulation by the Enemy to rob me of my sanctification and consecration, LORD, expose and frustrate it. In the name of Jesus.

8. Every power sitting on my prosperity and peace, LORD, unseat and disgrace it. In the name of Jesus.

9. LORD, release upon me now the power to fill my heart with Your Words always and stay undefiled. In the name of Jesus.

10. I reject and cancel every decree or anointing to be and remain a local champion. In the name of Jesus.

11. God of all grace, bring out the star in me and cause it to shine brightly. In the name of Jesus.

12. In my calling and pursuits in life, LORD, clothe me with the garment of honour and dignity. In the name of Jesus.

13. Spirit of excellence, possess my life for me to distinguish myself in all my endeavours. In the name of Jesus.

14. I decree that my star shall never sink but shine brightly as a shining light that shineth unto the perfect day. In the name of Jesus.

15. Wonderful LORD, I thank You for answering these prayers by fire. In the name of Jesus.

PRAYER 40

MAKE ME YOUR PECULIAR TREASURE, O LORD!

BIBLE VERSE: Exodus 19:5

INTRODUCTION

God is the Creator of heaven and earth and all things in them including human beings. The Bible says the creation of man and all creatures was good (Genesis 1:31). God states in His Word that human beings were created for His glory and praise (Jeremiah 13:11). Unfortunately, the praise, love, and trust God desired in the human beings He created were lost when the first people gave their hearts to the serpent (Devil) and incurred the wrath of God.

However, Noah found favour with God through obedience and right living. God demonstrated His special relationship in His dealing with Noah. While the whole world was destroyed due to gross wickedness, Noah and his family were preserved as peculiar treasures of God to repopulate the world. In the process of time, God began to relate to some people in a special way, which established their peculiarity. They became treasures to God. For example, Abraham, Joseph, Moses, David, and Jesus Christ, to mention but a few, became peculiar treasures to God by the special way He related to them. God promised the Israelites would be His peculiar people if they dwelt in obedience and right living (Exodus 19:5).

The criteria for anyone to become a peculiar treasure to God, which include the new birth experience, love, obedience, faith in God and right living will be fulfilled through the work of the Holy Spirit in human lives and prayers. Hence, through these prayers, we must seek to reach out to God for Him (by His Spirit) to change our "passive" spiritual content into an "active" response to His demand from us to love, obey and live right. That way, we will be honoured. I prophesy that the truth of God shall hit us into doing away with our distinctive behaviour or character to follow the footsteps of Jesus Christ and become God's peculiar treasures. In the mighty name of Jesus Christ.

PRAYER POINTS:

1. My Father, my Creator, I thank You for creating me for Your praise. Receive my quality praise and adoration today. In the name of Jesus.

2. I plead the blood of Jesus Christ and soak all mine, as well as myself in the blood. In Jesus' name.

3. Holy Ghost fire and blood of Jesus Christ, separate me from the curse of disobedience operating on my foundation. In the name of Jesus.

4. Every wicked spirit assigned to rob me of the will of God for life, you are a liar. Fall into the fire of God and die! In the name of Jesus.

5. LORD, make evil devices of household witchcraft to fall back upon their heads and backfire. In the name of Jesus.

6. I bind any satanic power assigned to hinder my progress in becoming a peculiar treasure to God. Die by the fire of God. In the name of Jesus.

7. Every evil voice rising against the glory of God for my life, be silenced forever. In Jesus' name.

8. Holy Ghost fire, destroy every garment of reproach in my life. In the name of Jesus.

9. My potentials come out of the grave and captivity. In the name of Jesus.

10. I command every disease-carrying parasites producing sickness in my body to come out of your hiding places and die. In the name of Jesus.

11. I break every curse of untimely death in my life and family. In the name of Jesus.

12. O LORD, my God, feed me with the food of the champions. In the name of Jesus.

13. O LORD, take me now to Your destination for my life, which is to become a peculiar treasure to You. In the name of Jesus.

14. LORD, establish Your breakthrough in my life to silence my adversaries forever. In the name of Jesus.

15. LORD, I thank You for answering my prayers by Your fire. In the name of Jesus.

PRAYER 41

EXALT MY HORN WITH HONOUR, O LORD!

BIBLE VERSES: *Psalm 89:17; 112:9*

INTRODUCTION

By definition, to "exalt" is to "dignify" or "regard specially." A "horn" is an important part of an animal and the symbol of its power. To "honour" is to "reverence" or to "respect specially." Therefore, to pray that the LORD exalts your horn with honour is to have the LORD treat you as important, have special regard, respect or praise for you with a view to receiving God's blessings continually.

The original plan of God was for all human beings to occupy a special position of honour before Him different from other creatures. At the time of creation, God put everything in place for human beings to enjoy His special honour and blessings (Genesis 1:27, 28). This special position of glory was lost by the first man Adam (Genesis 3:11-24). The glory was eventually restored by Jesus Christ (Romans 5:12). The restoration came out of God's love for the world and can be claimed by believing in and freely accepting the salvation that came through Jesus Christ (1 Thessalonians 5:9).

In Psalm 89 and 112, the psalmist recognizes God as the source of all power, strength, glory, honour, and blessings. He gives them to the upright who fear Him and delight in His commandments. Therefore, it is necessary in the following prayers to deal with every form of hindrance in our lives and, indeed, become the righteousness of God in Christ Jesus (2 Corinthians 5:21). That way, we can enjoy the heritage of the upright to the fullest. Therefore, I prophesy that all the onslaught of satanic and generational powers over your life shall be destroyed. Your righteousness will spring forth and go before you. Your horn will be exalted with honour. In Jesus' mighty name. Amen.

PRAYER POINTS:

1. Omnipotent and gracious God, I give You praise and honour for all You have done for me through this programme. May Your most holy name be glorified forever. In the name of Jesus.

2. I plead the precious blood of Jesus Christ. I cover myself and all that belongs to me with the blood. In the name of Jesus.

3. Holy Ghost fire, ignite my prayers today. In the name of Jesus.

4. Foundational powers of my father's house contending with the salvation of my soul be uprooted by the fire of God. In the name of Jesus.

5. LORD, by Your powerful blood, flush out of my system all the satanic food I ate in the dream to contaminate my spiritual life. In the name of Jesus.

6. Evil words in the form of arrows fired into my life by agents of the dark kingdom, backfire and boomerang on them. In Jesus' name.

7. Power of the accuser to block my glory from shining, expire by fire. In the name of Jesus.

8. Power of shame and dishonor in my life, die by the fire of God. In the name of Jesus.

9. Holy Ghost fire, consume any name or appellation that identifies me as evil or a child of reproach. In the name of Jesus.

10. LORD, cause the seed of righteousness, which is Your sanctification sown into my life to grow into a mighty tree. In the name of Jesus.

11. O LORD, anoint me with the power to walk before You and be perfect. In the name of Jesus.

12. O LORD, by Your mighty hands, draw me out of the valley of defeat and bring me onto the mountain of success and honour. In the name of Jesus.

13. My Father and My God, in the crowd of life, single me out for Your honour. In the name of Jesus.

14. O LORD, by Your divine will and what makes You Almighty, take me from where I am now to where I am welcome, loved, accepted, honoured, and rewarded. In the name of Jesus.

15. Wonderful LORD, I thank You for answering these prayers by fire and for the realm of honour in which you have placed me. In the name of Jesus.

PRAYER 42

LEAD AND GUIDE ME UNTO GREATER HEIGHTS, O LORD!

BIBLE VERSE: Psalm 31:3(b)

INTRODUCTION

By "greater heights," we mean "the higher realm of a place or position." Also, "to lead and guide" is "to direct or be in control of the movement of another." Hence, to pray the LORD leads and guides unto greater heights is for the LORD to direct or be in control of your ways, actions, and movements unto a higher realm or position. It is, and will continue to be an important prayer, as long as you remain alive.

"Progress" is the evidence of a good life, while "stagnation" is the evidence of a bad or unsatisfactory life. Believers in Christ are expected to continually make progress in their spiritual and physical lives. They should be aware of the fact that progress is good and "divine," meaning it comes from God. On the other hand, "stagnation" is bad and an instrument of torment from Satan. The realisation of this fact keeps believers constantly appraising their situation and taking positive steps to deal with anything that is unacceptable to them.

For the LORD to successfully lead and guide us unto greater heights, we must trust Him absolutely (Psalm 37:3), commit our ways, vocations, and possessions, etc. to Him (Psalm 37:5), as well as get and exalt His wisdom and understanding (Proverbs 4:7, 8), among other things. In light of the foregoing, it is appropriate that the LORD (the source of progress and greater heights) is entreated to be in total control of our lives for promotion to come to pass. Therefore, I prophesy that every power of stagnation in your life shall be consumed by the fire of God. You shall make good progress to greater heights . In Jesus' mighty name. Amen.

PRAYER POINTS:

1. LORD, God Almighty, I thank You and honour Your wonderful name for the abundance of Your grace, strength, and blessings in my life. May Your most holy name be praised forever.

2. I plead the precious blood of Jesus Christ and cover all that belongs to me and myself with the blood. In the name of Jesus.

3. Satanic embargo erected against my progress and prosperity, be dismantled by the thunder fire of God. In the name of Jesus.

4. Enemies of my success and joy, be disgraced. In the name of Jesus.

5. Holy Ghost fire, chase out every power of shame and disgrace in my life. In the name of Jesus.

6. LORD, frustrate the tokens of liars in my life. In the name of Jesus.

7. Any aspect of my life that is open to satanic manipulation, LORD, seal it with the blood of Jesus.

8. LORD, instruct and teach me in the way I should go and guide me with Your eyes. In Jesus' name.

9. LORD, take me to higher heights I have not known before in my spiritual and physical life. In the name of Jesus.

10. Because You are my refuge and fortress, LORD, keep me safe. In the name of Jesus.

11. I decree that nothing shall make me fear again. In the name of Jesus.

12. I shall be used for signs and wonders. The joy of the LORD shall be my strength. In Jesus' name.

13. Objects of my joy and happiness shall not cause me pain and sorrow. In the name of Jesus.

14. I shall be far from oppression and terror shall not come near me. In the name of Jesus.

15. I shall grow in grace and increase in the power and strength of the LORD. In the name of Jesus.

16. Wonderful LORD, I thank You for answering these prayers. In the name of Jesus.

PRAYER 43

REFINE ME AS GOLD FOR A RIGHTEOUS SERVICE TO YOU, O LORD!

BIBLE VERSE: Malachi 3:3 (NKJV)

INTRODUCTION

Gold and silver are chemical elements. They are precious metals of high value obtained after serious refining has been carried out and from which valuable and precious materials are made. To be refined as gold and silver is to pass through the spiritual purification fire of the LORD. This is done for definite cleansing and preparation, so you can be a new, precious instrument of service.

Every believer in Christ is expected at one point or the other on the Christian journey to have this encounter with the LORD – either at the point of salvation or thereafter as Isaiah did: "Then one of the seraphim flew to me, having in his hand a live coal which he had taken with the tongs from the altar. And he touched my mouth with it and said: Behold this has touched your lips; Your iniquity is taken away, and your sin purged" (Isaiah 6:6-7, NKJV). It is noteworthy to say that Isaiah's response to the encounter was to submit entirely to God's service.

The truth is that whenever this kind of encounter takes place, it will never be business as usual. All fears are gone; boldness comes in; vision becomes clearer, and service to God becomes pure, sincere, and enticing. Hence, these targeted prayers will be offered for the desired and expected experience. I prophesy, therefore, that by the operation of the power and fire in His Word, the LORD shall pass you through His refining fire now, deliver you from every impediment, and refine you for righteous service unto Himself. In Jesus' mighty name. Amen.

PRAYER POINTS:

1. Mighty and awesome God, I worship and adore You for what You are set to do in this month's programme. In the name of Jesus.

2. I plead the precious blood of Jesus Christ for cleansing and total coverage. In the name of Jesus.

3. Conspiracies of darkness over my prayers today, scatter by fire. In the name of Jesus.

4. Holy Ghost fire, destroy the generational powers of my father's house assigned to frustrate my calling. In the name of Jesus.

5. Ancestral covenants of idolatry attacking the foundation of my calling, break and be nullified by the blood of Jesus Christ.

6. Holy Ghost fire, uproot every seed of manipulation, oppression, and suppression planted into my life at birth. In the name of Jesus.

7. Whatever the plan of the dark kingdom for the demonic attack in my dream, LORD, frustrate and wipe it out. In the name of Jesus.

8. O LORD, arise in Your power and fire and consume every instrument of darkness planted in and around my family. In the name of Jesus.

9. LORD, arrest every strongman and strongwoman of my father's house and cause all my inheritance to be returned to me by fire. In the name of Jesus.

10. LORD, pass me through Your purification fire now and bring me out as gold. In the name of Jesus.

11. LORD, withdraw me by fire from every activity or assignment that stands to hinder my salvation and service to You. In the name of Jesus.

12. LORD, let the joy of Your salvation fill my heart continually. In the name of Jesus.

13. LORD, cause Your seeds of righteousness and peace to be sown into my life. Let them grow into mighty trees. In the name of Jesus.

14. LORD, equip me with Your power and instruments to serve You righteously, faithfully, and joyfully to the end. In the name of Jesus.

15. LORD, I thank You most sincerely for answering these prayers and delivering me by fire. In the name of Jesus.

PRAYER 44

GUIDE ME WITH YOUR COUNSEL CONTINUALLY, O LORD

BIBLE VERSES: Psalm 73:24a; Isaiah 58:11a (NKJV)

INTRODUCTION

"To guide with counsel continually" is "to direct with advice on a regular basis." Therefore, to be guided continually with the LORD's counsel is to be directed regularly by the LORD's advice in everything that pertains to your well-being.

The LORD desires to guide all His children with counsel continually (Isaiah 58:11a). God does this through His written laws and constant messages given directly by the Holy Spirit to believers or through His messengers. It is very sad to note that many times, His counsel often falls on deaf ears and the people get snared by many things (Isaiah 42:22). Every child of God (believer in Christ) must keep in focus this promise of God. We must study and meditate on the scriptures regularly (Joshua 1:8); listen to God's voice; strive to obey, be doers of the Word (James 1:22), and in constant prayer.

In light of the above, the following prayers are centered on this vital aspect of the life of the believer. I prophesy that every obstacle to the LORD's total direction in your life shall be dismantled. The LORD shall guide you with His counsel continually. In Jesus' mighty name. Amen.

PRAYER POINTS:

1. Omnipotent, omniscient, and omnipresent God, I bless and honour Your most holy name for the wonderful work You are doing in my life.

2. I plead the blood of Jesus Christ for cleansing and total coverage. In the name of Jesus.

3. Anywhere I have been hindering myself, O LORD, rescue me now. In the name of Jesus.

4. Every plan of the dark kingdom to stagnate my life, be nullified by the blood of Jesus. In Jesus' name.

5. Any frustration programmed into my life, lose your hold and be chased out. In the name of Jesus.

6. In the power of the Holy Spirit, I move beyond every limitation set by the Enemy. In the name of Jesus.

7. Pull down in disgrace all those who are planning to pull me down. In the name of Jesus.

8. Let the ears of my understanding be opened now, O LORD, and give me the capacity to hear and obey Your voice. In the name of Jesus.

9. Every fishless water in my life, LORD, command it to dry up and deliver me from fruitless labour. In Jesus' name.

10. I refuse to listen to satanic counsel. On the contrary, I delight to hear the LORD whose counsel shall stand in my life. In the name of Jesus.

11. O LORD, release to me now Your instructions or counsel for my success in life. In the name of Jesus.

12. LORD, wherever my human helpers are in this world, show them my picture and cause them to locate me. In the name of Jesus.

13. LORD, turn all former disappointments in my life into appointments. Turn my weeping into tears of joy. In the name of Jesus.

14. LORD, make my heart perfect before you and cause Your righteousness to sustain me. In the name of Jesus.

15. LORD, I thank You for answering these prayers by Your fire. In the name of Jesus.

DELIVERANCE AND HEALING PRAYERS

PRAYER 45

CANCEL THE PLAN AND MARK OF THE ENEMY OVER Y MY LIFE, O LORD!

BIBE VERSE: Psalm 140: 8.

INTROUCTION

A 'plan' is an intension; a proposed means of achieving something while a 'mark' is a stain on something. The enemy is anyone who is hostile, opposed or seeking to harm another person. To pray that the LORD cancels the plan and mark of the enemy in one's life, therefore, is to ask for divine intervention in frustrating that which the enemy is seeking to do.

The desire of the enemy to oppose, reproach or harm another is greatly enhanced by the presence of a mark or stain on the life of the victim. A mark on a person will facilitate easy identification by other dark kingdom powers to perpetrate or help to execute the plan of the enemy in the life of such a person. The plan and mark of the enemy in one's life can manifest in the following respects:

- Plan and mark of poverty; failure and defeat; shame and disgrace; stagnation, limitation or frustration; sickness or disease; untimely death; unfruitfulness, etc.

The LORD, cancelling the plan and mark of the enemy will be a three-staged affair. Firstly, He will expose the plan and mark of the enemy by the power of His word and Spirit. Secondly, He will cancel the plan and remove the mark by His precious blood. Thirdly, He will set free and release by His Spirit the blessings that are caged away by the enemy.

The story of Job in the Bible presents us with a good illustration. Satan's plan was to make Job miserable, sin and fall out of God's favour. He put the mark of terrible sickness upon him but by the mercy and power of the LORD, Job did not sin or fall. At the end he received healing and manifold blessings (Jb.2: 10-12; 42:12). Our adversary, satan together with his demons and human agents will do everything possible to re-live Job's predicament in human beings especially believers in Christ. In recognition of this fact, it is very important to offer fire prayers to God for Him to cancel and wipe out the plan and mark of the enemy in our lives. I prophesy, therefore, that the plan or counsel of the enemy in your life and family shall not stand nor come to pass in Jesus Name. The LORD shall turn around your breakdown to breakthrough, in Jesus Mighty Name, Amen.

PRAYER POINTS:

1. O LORD my Father, I thank You for Your mighty presence in my life and situation.

2. I plead the Blood of Jesus and cover myself and all that belong to me with the blood, in the name of Jesus.

3. LORD, clothe me and my prayers today with Your fire, in the name of Jesus.

4. Foundational powers assigned to monitor my life for evil, be paralyzed, impotent and die by fire, in the name of Jesus.

5. Satanic manipulation and misrepresentation of my confidence in God, be frustrated, in the name of Jesus.

6. Spirits of failure, disappointment and rejection, my life is not your candidate, die by fire, in the name of Jesus.

7. Wasters in my life and family be wasted by fire, in the name of Jesus

8. Every satanic crowd gathered to mock me, be disgraced and scattered, in the name of Jesus.

9. LORD, destroy every power and device of the wicked in my life and family, in the name of Jesus.

10. Every plan and mark of the enemy in my life, be cancelled and wiped out by the Blood of Jesus Christ, in Jesus name.

11. Arrow of affliction fired by satanic spiritual consultant into my life or endeavours, come out of my life, return to your sender and backfire, in the name of Jesus.

12. Release and restore unto me my kingdom blessings caged away by household enemies O LORD, in the name of Jesus.

13. My life, rise up from every form of breakdown and receive your breakthrough now, in the name of Jesus.

14. Those things which You have put in place to glorify Your name in my life, LORD, begin to manifest them now, in the name of Jesus.

15. LORD, I thank You for answering these prayers by fire, in the name of Jesus.

PRAYER 46

MOVING OUT THE MOUNTAIN IN MY LIFE AND CASTING SAME INTO THE SEA

BIBLE VERSE: Matthew 21:21 (NKJV)

INTRODUCTION

A mountain in the physical realm is a mass of land, which elevates to a great height. In the spiritual realm, a mountain represents stubborn problems that refuse to go away or defy solutions. To move mountains from your life means to make a great effort or to achieve amazing results in getting rid of the problems in your life.

If you are facing a problem that seems as big and immovable as a mountain, turn your eyes from the mountain and look unto Jesus Christ for more faith and power (Luke 17:5) to deal with it. Mountains, as well as problems, have ears (Micah 6:1) through the demons in charge. When spiritual authority is released on the demons and their operations, they are bound to surrender and literally vacate the problems they have created. Then deliverance miracles will follow.

The authority required to move mountains is executed when we pray. When believers pray mountain-moving prayers or any prayer whatsoever, it is better done through faith in God and the power of the Holy Spirit. Therefore, participants in this kind of prayer must be born again and filled with the Holy Spirit. No doubt, praying these prayers will move every mountain standing against us. As the LORD liveth and His spirit lives, I prophesy that these mountains, no matter what magnitude, shall hear the Word of the LORD, move out, and be cast into the sea. In Jesus' mighty name. Amen.

PRAYER POINTS:

1. Merciful and everlasting Father, I bless and honour Your most holy name for your faithfulness in my life. Receive all praise and adoration. In the name of Jesus.

2. I plead the precious blood of Jesus Christ and cover all that belongs to me and myself with the blood. In the name of Jesus.

3. Holy Ghost, incubate my life with Your fire for today's assignment. In the name of Jesus.

4. Blood of Jesus, wipe out every pattern of affliction in my generational line. In the name of Jesus.

5. Evil champion or strongman of my father's house holding my destiny in bondage, receive the judgment of self-destruction. In the name of Jesus.

6. I command every rage and rampage of the Enemy to freeze before me now. In the name of Jesus.

7. Arrow of sickness and infirmity fired into my life in the dream, come out and return to your senders. In the name of Jesus.

8. Blood of Jesus Christ, flush out every contamination in my body and blood. In the name of Jesus.

9. Blood of Jesus Christ, break and nullify every curse or counsel of untimely death hovering over my life. In the name of Jesus.

10. Mountains of problems in my life, I break your power and hold over my life. Be cast into the sea! In the name of Jesus.

11. I refuse to be submerged by the river of adversity. In the name of Jesus.

12. I shall not surrender to my problems; my problems shall surrender and vanish before me. In the name of Jesus.

13. Every battle prepared against my peace and progress, be frustrated and die. In the name of Jesus.

14. Abundant heavenly resources locate my life now. In the name of Jesus.

15. LORD, I thank You very much for answering these prayers and for the miracles that shall follow. In the name of Jesus.

PRAYER 47

RISE UP AND SCATTER EVIL CONSPIRACY IN MY LIFE AND FAMILY, O LORD!

BIBLE VERSE: Numbers 10:35

INTRODUCTION

"Evil conspiracy" can be explained in very simple words as "the unpleasant or harmful secret plans of enemies." These evil workers (enemies) are known by the way they carry out their evil works. They take the form of witches and wizards, demons and demonic agents, occult personalities or evil stubborn pursuers. They gather in secret places or covens where harmful plans and decisions are made. Such plans and decisions are carried out on innocent people by working together in groups or alone.

The LORD will be willing to rise up to fight and scatter evil conspiracy against His children when they humble themselves, have strong faith, trust, and confidence in the ability of the LORD to do it and call upon Him.

In our Bible verse today, Moses was aware of opposition on the Israelites' journey to the Promised Land. Hence, he called on the LORD to fight for them and scatter their enemies. In the same vein, as we are on the way to possess our earthly and eternal inheritance, Satan and his human agents (enemies) will surely engage in, and carry out an evil conspiracy against us to truncate the journey. They must be scattered unto desolation. For this reason, we must reach out to the LORD in prayers for Him to fight for us. Therefore, I prophesy that as you call upon the LORD today, He shall rise up and scatter every evil conspiracy against you and your family. In Jesus' mighty name. Amen.

PRAYER POINTS:

1. Everlasting and most powerful God, I give You honour and glory for the great work You are doing in my life and my family. Receive all praise and adoration forever. In the name of Jesus.

2. I plead the blood of Jesus Christ for cleansing of shortcomings in my life and total coverage. In the name of Jesus.

3. Holy Ghost, renew Your power, authority, and fire for today's assignment in me now! In the name of Jesus.

4. Powers from my foundation assigned against my spiritual and physical prosperity, your time is up. Die by fire! In the name of Jesus.

5. Satanic embargo or opposition built against my life to hinder my spiritual progress, be dismantled by the fire of God. In the name of Jesus.

6. Environmental powers assigned to frustrate my efforts as I work for God in my life, be exposed and destroyed by fire. In the name of Jesus.

7. Holy Ghost, chase out and destroy every spirit of fear and weakness in my life. In the name of Jesus.

8. Holy Ghost thunder, scatter all evil conspiracies against my life and turn their tables against them. In the name of Jesus.

9. LORD, set Your ambushes against all stubborn pursuers in my life and cause them to be wiped out. In the name of Jesus.

10. LORD, turn every instrument or weapon the stubborn enemies rely on to do their evil work in my life against them. In the name of Jesus.

11. LORD, lift up my hands upon my enemies for them to be cut off forever. In the name of Jesus.

12. LORD, drive out all illegal occupants on my land of destiny with Your fierce anger and terror. In the name of Jesus.

13. I shall fully enjoy the space the LORD has allocated to me on this planet earth to the end. In the name of Jesus.

14. LORD, scatter every evil conspiracy against Your church and dismantle their embargo. In the name of Jesus.

15. Wonderful LORD, I thank You for answering these prayers by fire. In the name of Jesus.

PRAYER 48

OPEN MY EYES TO SEE YOUR GREAT AND MIGHTY PLAN FOR MY LIFE, O LORD!

BIBLE VERSES: Jeremiah 33:2-3

INTRODUCTION

The word of the LORD to the prophet Jeremiah in our Bible verses and, indeed, to all the saints of God, is quite loaded in quality and substance. This fact is clearly evident in the privilege we have to call and the assurance of the sovereign God, not only to answer the call but also give revelation to His saints.

The truth is the LORD is willing and ready to answer our prayers and give us revelations. Through the inspiration of God's Spirit, Moses said: "The secret things belong unto the LORD our God; but those things which are revealed belong unto us" (Deuteronomy 29:29). The LORD does the revelation, but His saints must do the asking (Matthew 7:7). Invariably, the LORD's answer is always amazing and/or miraculous.

God is omniscient; He knows all things including His plans for His children. Therefore, to call on Him for a revelation of what He plans to do in our lives, no doubt, will commands immediate answer, which will also serve as a booster to our faith and trust in the LORD. Thus, these prayers are designed to provide the avenue to actualize the immutable counsel of the LORD for our lives.

I prophesy that every veil of darkness covering your dreams and visions shall be torn off. The LORD shall not only show you His great and mighty plan for your life but also bring the plans to fulfillment. In the mighty name of Jesus. Amen.

PRAYER POINTS:

1. Mighty and everlasting God, I bless and honour You for who You are and all You are doing in my life. Adoration and glory be to Your most holy name. In the name of Jesus.

2. I plead the blood of Jesus Christ and cover all that belongs to me and myself with the blood. In the name of Jesus.

3. Holy Ghost fire, fall upon me and ignite my prayers. In the name of Jesus.

4. Satanic veil of darkness covering my dreams and visions, be torn off. In the name of Jesus.

5. Spiritual blindness that entered my life through demonic manipulation, be wiped off by the blood of Jesus. In Jesus' name.

6. All anti-prosperity altars raised against my life, be dismantled by the fire of God. In the name of Jesus.

7. Every embargo or opposition built by the dark kingdom against the fulfillment of God's plan for my life and family, be dismantled by the fire of God. In the name of Jesus.

8. Holy Ghost, frustrate all the activities of star high-jackers and destiny diverters in my life. In the name of Jesus.

9. LORD, command Your warring angels to breakdown the strong room of household enemies in my life and make it desolate. In the name of Jesus.

10. LORD, open my eyes to see Your great and mighty goodness planned for my life. In the name of Jesus.

11. LORD, cause the storehouse of heaven to be opened and Your angels to release to me all the wealth and prosperity meant for my life. In the name of Jesus.

12. LORD, command Your glory for my life that is presently in the wrong hands to be returned to me now. In the name of Jesus.

13. Spirit and power of the living God, catapult me to the glorious destiny You planned for my life. In the name of Jesus.

14. The great and mighty plan of the great and mighty God for my life shall not be truncated by sin or flesh. In the name of Jesus.

15. My wonderful LORD, I thank You for Your answers to these prayers. In the name of Jesus.

PRAYER 49

WORK YOUR UNFORGETTABLE AND MARVELOUS WORK IN ME, O LORD

BIBLE VERSE: *Habakkuk 1:5*

INTRODUCTION

The LORD is the greatest and most marvelous worker. His work of creation, which stands out as a landmark and His redemptive work through Jesus Christ, among others, are clear testimonies to this fact. Even in people's physical lives, God remains the greatest in His works, which are rightly referred to as "miracles" because they are not explicable in terms of natural laws. God doing His unforgettable and marvelous work in you is the superlative manifestation of God's miracle in your life.

The unforgettable and marvelous work of God done in people's lives is the proof of God's faithfulness – whether it is in the area of salvation, healing, deliverance, prosperity or peace. Without a doubt, the Bible is designed to provide undisputed testimonies of God's great and marvelous work in the lives of His people.

The LORD's response to Habakkuk's question in the Bible verse and Isaiah's special encounter with the LORD (Isaiah 6:5-8), which marked a unique turning point in Isaiah's life, are testimonies of the LORD's willingness to do extraordinary work in the lives of the people. Asking the LORD to do this kind of work in you will, without doubt, be the wisest prayer at this point in time. Therefore, I prophesy that every hindrance to God in your life shall be removed by fire, so He can do His unforgettable and marvelous work in your life. In Jesus' mighty name. Amen.

PRAYER POINTS:

1. Almighty and all-powerful God, I give You glory for Your mighty works in my life. May Your most holy name be honoured and praised forever. In the name of Jesus.

2. I plead the precious blood of Jesus Christ and cover myself with the blood. In the name of Jesus.

3. Power and strength to be a warrior and not to worry, fall upon me now. In the name of Jesus.

4. As the battle axe of God, I decree destruction upon all ancestral or foundational powers working to undermine my prayers. In the name of Jesus.

5. Blood of Jesus, break and cancel any generational or verbal curse blocking the move of God in my life. In the name of Jesus.

6. O LORD, uproot by fire whatever is standing as a strange god or idol in my heart and preventing my true worship of You. In the name of Jesus.

7. LORD, bring into open shame and disgrace all the haters and despisers of Your great work in my life. In the name of Jesus.

8. Any of my blessings presently in the hands of dead relatives, come out of the grave and be restored to me now! In the name of Jesus.

9. LORD, carry out Your plan to lift Your hands against my adversaries and subdue them before me now. In the name of Jesus.

10. By the fire of God, I withdraw and claim back my glory in the hands of any household enemies. In the name of Jesus.

11. LORD, Your promise of provision and care for me shall be fulfilled without delay. In the name of Jesus.

12. LORD, heal and deliver me in any area that needs Your healing touch. In the name of Jesus.

13. LORD, transform me in any area that needs transformation. In the name of Jesus.

14. Your covenant of peace, prosperity, and protection in my life shall never be broken. In the name of Jesus.

15. LORD, I thank You for answering these prayers by Your fire. In the name of Jesus.

PRAYER 50

PULL DOWN EVERY SATANIC STRONGHOLD IN MY LIFE, O LORD!

BIBLE VERSE: *2 Corinthians 10:4 (AMP)*

INTRODUCTION

A stronghold is a place or means of protection, safety or refuge. A satanic stronghold is any hiding place or refuge for Satan and his agents to do their evil work. For God to pull down every satanic stronghold in your life, it means He will dismantle or tear down every hiding place or whatever enables Satan and his agents to execute their evil assignments in human lives.

Satanic strongholds can be built up and maintained in human lives through sin, curses, covenants, soul ties, familiar spirits or guardian spirits, devourers, wasters, and destroyers. The presence of any of the foregoing in human lives will provide the stronghold for Satan and his agents to accomplish their evil purposes. Some evil assignments of Satan, his demons, and human agents include retrogression and set-backs, slavery and servitude, poverty and wretchedness, affliction, sickness, and untimely death, among others.

The Bible warns all believers "not to be ignorant of his (satan's) devices" (2 Corinthians 2:11b). "Whom resist (Satan) steadfast in faith" (1 Peter 5:9a). These prayers are used to seek the LORD's intervention to fight the battle and pull down every stronghold of Satan. I prophesy, therefore, that the LORD shall arise and cause His hosts to pull down and dismantle every satanic stronghold in your life. In Jesus' mighty name. Amen.

PRAYER POINTS:

1. Mighty and everlasting Father, I give You praise and honour for Your faithfulness in my life.

2. I soak and cover myself and all that belongs to me with the blood of the Lord Jesus Christ.

3. Every weakness in my spiritual life that gives room to satanic strongholds in my life, Holy Ghost fire, consume it now. In the name of Jesus.

4. Every veil of darkness blocking my vision to provide room for satanic strongholds in my life, Holy Ghost, tear it off now! In the name of Jesus.

5. Foundational curse or covenant of retrogression and set back in my life, be uprooted by the fire of God. In the name of Jesus.

6. Every curse or covenant of untimely death in my life, be uprooted and broken by the fire of God. In the name of Jesus.

7. Every strongman in charge of keeping the gate of satanic strongholds in my life, be paralyzed and die by fire. In the name of Jesus.

8. LORD, command Your hosts to pull down and destroy whatever is standing as a satanic stronghold in my life and family. In the name of Jesus.

9. LORD, release Your weapon of war and destroy every satanic instrument or weapon fashioned against me and my family. In the name of Jesus.

10. LORD, by Your fire, command the release of all my prosperity, blessings, and breakthroughs that are being held up by satanic strongholds. In the name of Jesus.

11. I receive the power to tread upon serpents and scorpions, as well as every power of the Enemy from now on. In the name of Jesus.

12. LORD, build Your wall of fire around me to frustrate the agenda of Satan and his agents forever. In the name of Jesus.

13. LORD, hide me in Your strong tower, which is Your name and make me dwell there forever. In the name of Jesus.

14. From today, I refuse to be an object of shame or ridicule. I shall possess my possession. In the name of Jesus.

15. LORD, I thank You for answering these prayers by fire. In the name of Jesus.

PRAYER 51

UTTERLY CONSUME ALL WICKED PURSUERS IN MY LIFE WITH TERRORS, O LORD!

BIBLE VERSES: Psalm 73:18-19

INTRODUCTION

"Wicked pursuers" are agents of Satan and the dark kingdom with sinister motives. They bring evil, harmful afflictions, disasters, calamities, and all kinds of problems that cause sorrow and pain into the lives of their victims. Wicked pursuers also manipulate, hinder, oppress, and depress people at will to fulfill their covenant with Satan and his dark kingdom. The ultimate aim is to prevent their victims from attaining their God-given destiny and success.

The LORD Jesus Christ describes the functions of Satan (the head of all wickedness) as "The thief (who) cometh not, but for to steal, and to kill, and to destroy" (John 10:10a). He has been in the world from the beginning with this work and will continue as long as the world remains. The wicked pursuers operate in line with the directives they receive from

Satan. Their unsuspecting victims are left with the problem of knowing the origin of their problems and addressing them in the most appropriate manner.

God is the Almighty. He is the one "that frustrateth the tokens of the liars" (Isaiah 44:25a). Hence, through our prayers and faith in God and His power as testified by David in the Bible verse of today, God delivers us from the powers of the wicked pursuers, "for the battle is not yours, but God's" (2 Chronicles 20:15b). As we reach out to God on this matter in these prayers, I prophesy that the LORD GOD almighty shall arise, fight your battle, and utterly consume all wicked pursuers in your life with terror. In Jesus' mighty name. Amen.

PRAYER POINTS:

1. Almighty God, I bless and honour You for the abundance of Your grace upon my life. Receive all praise and adoration. In the name of Jesus.

2. I plead the blood of Jesus and cover myself, as well as all that belongs to me with the blood. In the name of Jesus.

3. Every doorway opened to the satanic invasion in my life, be closed permanently. In the name of Jesus.

4. Every device of manipulation and wickedness programmed into my life, be destroyed by the fire of God. In the name of Jesus.

5. Satanic designs of oppression against me in my dreams and visions, be frustrated by the blood of Jesus. In Jesus' name.

6. Any evil that has been done in my dream by wicked pursuers, blood of Jesus, cancel it. In the name of Jesus.

7. All organized warfare against my destiny and success, be disgraced by the terror of the LORD. In the name of Jesus.

8. Activators of afflictions, disasters, tragedies, and problems in my life and family, be destroyed by the fire of God. In the name of Jesus.

9. O God, arise in my situation. Fight for me and cause me to hold my peace. In the name of Jesus.

10. LORD, utterly consume with terror every wicked pursuer in my life and family. In the name of Jesus.

11. The rod of the wicked shall not fall upon my lot and my hands shall not touch evil. In the name of Jesus.

12. I recover by fire all that the Enemy stole or destroyed through wickedness. In the name of Jesus.

13. Spirit of success and excellence, fall upon my life now and take firm control forever. In the name of Jesus.

14. LORD, lay Your hand on me and move me safely into my divine destiny and success. In the name of Jesus.

15. Father LORD, I thank You most sincerely for answering these prayers by Your fire. In the name of Jesus.

PRAYER 52

SILENCE THE RAGE OF THE WICKED IN MY LIFE, O LORD!

BIBLE VERSE: (1 Samuel 2:9)

INTRODUCTION

To be in "rage" is to be "violently angry." "The wicked" is "one that is evil and does evil things continually." To pray that the LORD silences the rage of the wicked, therefore, is to ask for divine action against the unprovoked, violent anger of the evil ones against us.

The world is full of diverse forms of wickedness ranging from quiet but clever deception to violent or furious attacks or torment by one person on another due to hatred, opposition, rejection or provocation. The situation that led Hannah into the prayer of thanksgiving in the Bible verse of today is a typical example of the rage of the wicked. "And her adversary also provoked her sore" (1 Samuel 1:6).

Satan is at the head of all wickedness and those who do wickedly are his agents. Believers and, indeed, the church of God are the targets of the rage of the wicked. The attacks will always come from the enemies of our households, workplaces, businesses, religion or society to mention just a few. The ultimate desire of the wicked or evil ones is to ensure that through their rage, they frustrate God's covenant of peace and progress in the lives of their victims.

Like Hannah, it is appropriate to call on the LORD for divine action against every form of wickedness in our lives. Therefore, I prophesy that the LORD shall arise at your call and silence the rage of the wicked in your life and destiny. In Jesus' mighty name. Amen.

PRAYER POINTS:

1. Everlasting Father, the El-Shaddai, I praise and honour Your most holy name for Your faithfulness in my life. Receive all thanksgiving for Your works in my life through this programme. In the name of Jesus.

2. By the covenant of the blood of Jesus, I receive total cleansing and coverage. In the name of Jesus.

3. Put forth Your hands, O LORD, and touch my mouth for me to be filled with Your words and fire. In the name of Jesus.

4. I command every foundational power projecting the satanic agenda in my life to die by fire. In the name of Jesus.

5. Seeds of hatred, oppression, rejection, provocation, and defeat sown into my life and family by household enemies, be uprooted by fire and burnt to ashes. In the name of Jesus.

6. LORD, destroy every platform the enemies of my success and breakthrough are standing upon to fight me. In the name of Jesus.

7. Anywhere they gather together to oppress or torment my life, LORD, scatter them. In the name of Jesus.

8. Agents of oppression and discomfort in my life, be disgraced. In the name of Jesus.

9. What I love to do shall not become a snare for the wicked one to oppress my life. In the name of Jesus.

10. Invisible God, continue to be my strength and shield in the battles of life. In the name of Jesus.

11. LORD, overturn the reproach of the evil ones in my life and fill my mouth with songs of deliverance. In the name of Jesus.

12. LORD, silence forever every rage of the wicked one in my life and destiny. In the name of Jesus.

13. I shall triumph over all my adversaries and put them into open and permanent disgrace. In the name of Jesus.

14. LORD, break into pieces all the adversaries of Your church. In the name of Jesus.

15. LORD, I thank You for answering these prayers by fire. In the name of Jesus.

PRAYER 53

THERE SHALL BE SHOWERS OF BLESSING

BIBLE VERSES: *Ezekiel 34:26 – 30*

INTRODUCTION

A blessing is divine favour or heavenly provision, protection or reward. Every human blessing is always driven by God's Spirit. We are concerned here with the blessings that come by miracles through the action of God.

When an employer refuses to pay the wages the employees are entitled to or somebody decides to withhold payment for what is bought, such decisions can be overruled by divine intervention.

It is very important for believers to know the will of God in any situation they find themselves. Some of the situations can make believers cry or rejoice. Therefore, believers must know the will of God in

(a) sickness (Isaiah 53:4-5; 1 Peter 2:24); (b) danger (Psalm 23:4); (c) poverty or lack (2 Corinthians 8:9); (d) barrenness or unfruitfulness (Deuteronomy 7:13-14); (e) all-round prosperity and blessing (Ezekiel 34:26).

Since God's will for His children remains unchanged, it is always wise for the children (believers) to be conversant with His will in any given situation. This enables the believer to hold on in prayers reminding God of His Words or promises (Isaiah 55:11). Holding to God's Word in any given situation enables the quick performance of His promises (Jeremiah 1:12).

Note this well, however, that the Devil will always tell you to help yourself and forget God or make you tired of waiting for Him. Have absolute faith, trust, and patience for God to work in your life. God says, and I prophesy it into your life that at destruction and famine you will laugh (Job 5:22). As you remain faithful to God and His Word, you will receive the shower and abundance of His blessings. In Jesus' mighty name. Amen.

PRAYER POINTS:

1. My LORD and Redeemer, I thank You because You will open Your heavens for my sake now.

2. Holy Spirit, draw me unto the throne of grace for my shower of blessings. In the name of Jesus.

3. By the blood of Jesus and Your mercy, forgive every shortcoming in my obedience, faith, trust, and patience for You. In the name of Jesus.

4. Satanic power attacking the channel of God's blessings in my life, collide with the Rock of Ages and break to pieces. In the name of Jesus.

5. Every conspiracy of darkness against my finances, scatter by the fire of God. In the name of Jesus.

6. Holy Ghost Fire, give me my blessings that are being held up in the demonic storehouse. In the name of Jesus.

7. My Father and my maker, I need the miracle of Your provisions. In the name of Jesus.

8. Holy Ghost, expose and consume every bait of Satan in and around me by Your fire. In the name of Jesus.

9. My divine blessings, what are you doing in the storehouse of the Devil? Come out by fire! In the name of Jesus.

10. Holy Spirit, frustrate the plans of the wicked for my family's blessings. In the name of Jesus.

11. In all areas of the Devil's deceits, LORD, fight for me and disgrace him. In the name of Jesus.

12. Season of dryness in my life, home, and family, expire! In the name of Jesus.

13. Cause the shower of Your blessings to come down upon me and my family, O LORD. In the name of Jesus.

14. What You have given to me as blessings – children, money, prosperity, etc., shall not be used to destroy me. In the name of Jesus.

15. LORD, I thank You for Your answer to my prayers and the flow of the blessings. In the name of Jesus.

BOOK BY THE SAME AUTHOR

Do you need prosperity, deliverance, and healing? Is your life stuck and going nowhere? Would you like a miraculous breakthrough?

In this life, we experience crippling blows to our plans and future. Things don't turn out the way we hoped and prayed. And trouble seems to be everywhere. Whether quiet and clever or open and violent, evil affects us all, and the dark kingdom blocks our prosperity, while creating confusion in our lives. Its goal is destruction and chaos. Can you halt Satan's attacks and command prosperity, peace, and freedom for you and your family?

Prayer Guide for Spiritual Exploits will kindle the fire of prayer in you. It will wake you up to overthrow the Enemy's schemes, so you can enjoy unlimited spiritual health and wealth. Filled with powerful healing and deliverance prayers, as well as prophetic declarations, this energetic guide leads you in prayers that will preempt the Enemy's attacks and forever change your life.

For a few minutes each day, say these prayers with authority and experience divine intervention. Strongholds will come down, generational curses broken, and sicknesses healed. You will walk in victory and prosperity as the mighty power of God is unleashed in your life.

This book also includes:

- Scriptures for daily reading
- Discussions before every prayer point
- Power-packed prayers against witchcraft and destiny killers

www.ingramcontent.com/pod-product-compliance
Lightning Source LLC
Chambersburg PA
CBHW032032290426
44110CB00012B/775